# HISTORY OF WILLIAMSON COUNTY, ILLINOIS: FROM THE EARLIEST TIMES, DOWN TO THE PRESENT, 1876

Published @ 2017 Trieste Publishing Pty Ltd

ISBN 9780649604876

History of Williamson County, Illinois: From the Earliest Times, down to the Present, 1876 by Milo Erwin

Edited by Trieste Publishing Pty Ltd.
 Cover @ 2017

www.triestepublishing.com

**MILO ERWIN**

# HISTORY OF WILLIAMSON COUNTY, ILLINOIS: FROM THE EARLIEST TIMES, DOWN TO THE PRESENT, 1876

Trieste

# HISTORY

OF

# WILLIAMSON COUNTY

## ILLINOIS

From the Earliest Times, Down to the Present,

1876

With An Accurate Account of the Secession Movement,
Ordinances, Raids, Etc., Also, a Complete History of
Its "Bloody Vendetta," Including All Its Re-
condite Causes, Results, Etc., Etc.,

—BY—

## MILO ERWIN

Attorney at Law

---

"Mine be the friend, less frequent in his prayers,
Who makes no bustle with his soul's affairs,
Whose wit can brighten up a wintry day,
And chase the splenetic dull hours away."

---

MARION, ILLINOIS
1876

# BY WAY OF EXPLANATION.

"Not to know what happened before we were born is to remain always a child; for what were the life of man did we not combine present events with the recollections of past ages?" This, said Cicero many ages ago. No community is without a history, and, few, it will be agreed by those of you fortunate enough to peruse the following pages, have to offer such an interesting history as this one written now nearly forty years ago of Williamson county. Its author, Milo Erwin, was, in his time, one of the county's most eminent lawyers. Many stories are told about the excitement the publication of this book caused. It is now republished for the first time, and with no other intention whatsoever than to enlighten the present generation of the turbulent period through which this community has passed. In behalf of the well known families connected with the terrible vendetta which is here related it should be said that they are now among the best families in the community and some of the persons named are counted at present, good citizens who have lived down all odium that once attached to their names. The fact that there has in recent years been a great demand for copies of this rare work of which now

probably less than half a dozen copies are
in existence has led us to republish it. Without claiming any credit whatever except
that of preserving in a new edition this valuable portion of our county's interesting history, we have here reproduced the book
practically word for work just as its author
wrote it, even following as far as practical
the general make up and style of typo-
graphy. It is a piece of writing well done
and as Charles Dickens would say, "our
unhallowed hands shall not disturb it."

HAL W. TROVILLION,
EDITOR OF THE NEWS,
December 1st, 1914.          Herrin, Illinois.

## Prefatory Address to the Young Men
## of Williamson County.

GENTLEMEN:

I have now written you a history of your own county, to show you the advantages of civilization, and to give you contentment. It is a "home-spun" book written by a "home-spun" author.

The state of society which I have depicted is fast fading from the memory of men, and will soon live only in history. You come upon the scenes of life at an eventful and glorious age of the world, when the opportunities for individual progress are so hopeful. We are the citizens of a common country, and share an undivided interest in her weal or woe; and it may be well for us to look back to the past, on the bright side of misfortune; but we must trust to the future, "Though gloomy and cheerless,

    Prowls the dark past like a ghost at our
          back."

We have lived in the shadow of the gray hairs of our fathers. They have battled long and well to give us a country to live in, and we are the rich inheritors of all the glorious results of their self-denial and patriotic devotion. Let us prove ourselves worthy of the high destiny for which they offered themselves a sacrifice to common dangers

and privations, by living honorable lives,
and showing to the world that with affection we cherish their acts and hallow their
memories.

They have lived to see the forest con-
verted into farms, and have nobly done their
part, settling the country and serving it in
military and civil capacities. They have left
us a great country, and now the duty of defense and preservation rests on us. As a
slight repayment for the liberty we enjoy,
let us ever stand ready to bear arms in defense of this grand country, in which we
have the hapiness to live, against external
and internal foes.

The hope of the country is in its young
men; and the hope of the young men is in the
strength of their integrity. Live temper-
ately, deal justily, and respond in every act
to the demands of conscience, and you will
have an even chance in the human race for
worldly prosperity and recognition.

You owe the duty of education and moral
culture to yourselves; to your neighbors fair
dealing and generosity. Our best friends
are at home, those who would do most for
us. They dwell by our sides, and if they are
our best friends we should be theirs; and
if we are we should show it, for in this lies
the power of friendship to bless or curse us.
These cords of friendship should be treated
delicately, and never be broken by fretful,
surly and hateful means. Let it be your
constant object to strengthen, build up and
inprove home folks, for this is the source of
our sweetest pleasures and best life. Into

this fountain let no bitter dregs of poison drop. Keep it clear and pure. The miseries of broken friendships plead with you to preserve a high respect for your neighbors at all price. Be true to them if you are false to all else on earth beside. In this view the growth of our country becomes sublime and of surpassing interest.

While other countries have their traditions to excite them to patriotism, we have the inspiration coming from the names of illustrious men to summon us to great trials and duties.

There is no reason why a community of as intelligent, honest and industrious a people as ours, should not live in peace and plenty. We must learn to denounce crime and punish criminals, and not stand ready to applaud them. Our criminals must lay down their arms, for there never can be peace as long as they sleep on them. The law must be enforced; without this, life will be unsafe and property invaded. Young men, help build up a healthy public sentiment against crime.

I retain as much affection for my mother country as a common origin inspires; yet I feel a painful revulsion when making a comparison between this county and some others in this state. And I appeal to you by every bond that will bind a good man to his social duty, by every consideration that will awaken a love of county or stir your pride of race, to live true to the highest, purest and most lasting interest of your county.

In writing this book I proposed to myself, as a maxim, that no man should be able
from its pages to tell what political party I
belong to; so impartially have I tried to write
it. And I hope I will not   assume the imputation of vanity when I say I believe I have
done so. And if I have written a thought or
expression calculated to sting the pride or
wound the heart of any honest man, I stand
in the way of his indulgence, for I have not
intended to.  No historical work has ever
been written, or ever will be, but that some
defects can be found in it, especially dealing
with events so recent as our Vendetta must
the historian lay himself open to these stric-
tures.  I have aimed to give as full and fair
account of our history, with the more recon-
dite causes of Vendetta, as I was able.  I
was so happy as not to displease my friends
with my first attempts at writing, but I dare
not raise my hopes so high now.  I know
that many irate and insulting critics will
bugle about this book, and say that my learn-
ing is easily gleaned. I will admit that, and
ask them to follow my example. The choice
of subjects is not at my discreation, so that
the grace and style of my composition is
not such as I could wish. As I have not un-
dertaken to invent facts, of course I had to
draw from many sources, especially   our
old men and the members of the Vendetta.
And I have tried to eliminate from the mass
of facts such as would be most interesting to
read and remember. I do not want to be accused of supposing that all heroism, humanity, generosity and chivalry is in this county,

and that all cruelty, rapacity, cowardice and
ferocity is among our neighbors. I believe
it to be true, and shall try to show that while
our Vendetta has been signalized by some
deeds disgraceful to human nature, the general behavior of our people has been such
as would do honor to mankind, and exalt the
prestige of our name.

That Liberty, Progress, Knowledge, Virtue and Peace may be the lot and destiny of
our people, is as much the fervent aspiration
as it is the consoling faith of

MILO ERWIN.

Marion, Ill., December 1st, 1876.

# THE HISTORY

—OF—

# WILLIAMSON COUNTY
## ILLINOIS.

---

## OF THE COUNTRY.

In 1512, Juan Ponce de Leon discovered
Florida, and the whole of our country was
claimed by Spain, by virtue of this discov-
ery, under the name Florida. The earliest
settlement was made in Illinois in 1680, and
two years afterward, the Mississippi having
been discovered by DeSoto, the French took
formal possession of the valley of the Mississippi, and in honor of Louis, King of
France, named in Louisiana. Soon after that
event this country began to be called the Illinois country, after a powerful tribe of Indians by that name. In 1763, by a treaty between England and France, this country became an English province, and remained as
such until it was surrendered to the United
States by the John Jay treaty in 1796.

—F 2

After the formal surrender of the North-west Territory to the United States, it was divided into five counties. The portion of the Territory in which Williamson county is embraced belonged to St. Clair county, with Kaskaskia as the county seat, in which condition it remained until 1809, when Illinois was organized into a Territory proper. Congress appointed a Governor over this Territory who, in order to execute the laws, was authorized to lay out the Territory into counties, which he did; and this portion of the Territory which had hitherto been part of St. Clair county, now fell into Gallatin county, where it belonged until Illinois was admitted into the Union in 1818, and Franklin county was taken off the west side of Gallatin. In 1839, Franklin county was divided by act of the Legislature, and the southern half called Williamson county. Under the Territorial government the Governor appointed the magistrates and other officers, and they had to be freeholders; but since the admission of the State they have all been elected, and property qualification abolished.

Williamson county is twenty-four miles long from east to west, and eighteen from north to south. It contains 432 square miles, and 276,480 acres of land. At present it is divided into twelve townships and fifteen voting precincts. The surface of the county is level, with the exception of some rough land along its south side. It is traversed by a copious supply of large streams and their tributaries. The Saline and Crab Orchard run the whole length through the south side, and Big Muddy River cuts deeply into the northwest corner, while Pond and Lake Creeks wind and twist themselves along the northern portion until they come to what is known as the Scatters of Pond Creek, which is a swamp for two miles in extent, covered with tall grass, where the creek soaks lazily along among the tufts of grass, finally forming a stream again and emptying into Big Muddy.

There are ten separate and distinct veins of bituminous coal in this county, which spreads out and underlies three-fourths of its surface, and in dozens of places crops out where it can be cheaply and easily mined; and the veins average nine feet in thickness. No country on the globe is better supplied with coal than this county.

When our fathers came here, they found these vast, silent, virgin plains unclaimed, untouched, untilled, hedgeless, free to all. Field-like in wastes, yet fertile, awaiting, full of charms and loveliness, the smiling face of man. On entering the county from the east side an immense floe stretched westward beyond the reach of vision; the burning landscape was gashed with deep ravines, against whose rocky throats an old tree formed a pent-house on this silent main for travelers against rain and tempest. No sound broke nature's solemn repose. The summer breeze rocked itself to sleep in the elm boughs, and only the waning moon seemed alive, as it climbed up a cloudless sky, passing starry sentinels, whose mighy challenge was lost in the vast vortexes of blue, as they paced the ceaseless rounds in the canopy of constellations. Many a beautiful little lake, without a ripple, lay hid in the tall grass, reflecting the birds that passed over them, and from their clear bosom gave back the polished beauty of the heavens above.

The northern and southern portions of the county were well timbered; but the central was a vast barrens, without a shrub, except on the streams; but is now heavily timbered. There are nine beautiful little prairies in the county, averaging about three square miles each, the edges of which were studded with low trees—crab apples, hawthorns, red buds, etc., which bloomed in the spring, making most romantic scenery. Many of these little groves remain to this day, with Nature's own rich festooning hung, and afford a splendid retreat for picnics. But there is nothing in a tree alone to please; it is the variety which Nature gives that makes the complex emotions and beautiful sensations in men. She has been profuse. She spreads blossoms over the face of the country. Flowers hang like jewels from boughs; but she puts on no unnecessary paint. More sweetness would cloy the palate, more beauty would pale the sight. There is no room for a man to call up a more delightful theme. The trees had a gorgeous drapery of flowers and coniferous vines, and the horizontal limbs rose by regular stagings, one above the other, where the rural dcities revealed in their own sylvan solitudes, wearing their wreaths twined by the rosy fingers of Romana, and the spicy odors swept up the drowsy upland all day  from the forest and prairie meadows, while the air was lifting clustering rings of dark clouds above. This was a lovely home for the Red Man, where the dews of Egypt killed roses and vines for him, and Nature, with her sweet influence, taught him to love and adore the Great Spirit in this fair haven of happiness and repose, too pure and stainless to be sullied by immorality. But Nature is not lavish; she spreads her white robes in the spring, and  reserves  her  red until autumn.

When our fathers came here, they found

the grass higher than their heads, and for
twenty years it was the best range that man
ever saw, until the farmers stopped the
hunters from burning the woods. When this
was done, the leaves killed the grass, and
up came the bushes. Some of this tall grass
grows on the scatters of Pond Creek every
year. They found a great deal of wet land,
or swamps. On account of the vegetation
growing so thick and rank, the water could
not run off fast. Our fathers found herbs
for medicine and beverage. There was
savey and thyme for broth, sage for sausage,
pink-root for worms, and worm-wood for
bruises, flowers for bouquets, and apples
for friends. In these rude solitudes was
the bright golden paw-paw apple, six inches
long and three in diameter, mellow
and sweet, but not very delicious. There
were ferns and water-lilies with long deep
green, shiny leaves standing near the virgin
poplar, with its cluster of leaves waving
against the blue sky, which sent out its
shady radiance like the borealis waves its
ghastly banners over a midnight sky. These
prairies ripple and glitter yet; but wherever
civilized man has put his foot, it has left its
print, and now wild briars, thorns and
thistles have grown up to choke out the
sweet blossoms which once bloomed over this
county. The forests are cut down in many

places, and rich mansions point their steeples
and spires up to heaven. Rich exotic and
tropical plants mingle their patrician odors
with the tints of our native blue-bells and
ladies' slippers.

But some of our fathers came here when
the glad sound of waters was not heard;
when the streams were locked in the icy
shackles of winter; when the grass lay buried beneath autumnal snows; when the winds
went wailing over the desolate brightness,
and the cypress, with its countless, interlac-
ed branches of hoary gray, stood up like a
line of giant ghosts, an aspect of desolation
and death. When they came here they found
no monuments of past greatness; no Coliseum lay in a pile of ruins; no Obelisk of
Sesotris pointed its alabaster finger to the
eternal source of light; no Pyramids frown-
ed down upon them; no battle-scars were
seen. There were no towering evergreens,
Oriental bowers, or statuary. It was a virgin land, with delightful nooks, shady retreats, creeping vines, wrestling amid the
forest of perpetual green, and barren districts, with the storm-brand of ages on their
breast. It was a new land. Her greatness
was all in the future—her history yet to be
made and written, except where it had been
written by Nature's legible hand. It was a
land of trees; a land of flowers; a land of

plains and brooks and vales; a land in whose
dark, deep dells of the garden of Memory
lies embedded; in whose blessed retreats the
aged pioneer can refresh and   strengthen
himself, and drink in   anew   the   pearly
streams of happiness that rippled along its
sunlit banks; a land where imagination can
wing her proud flight from lofty realms to
realms more lofty still; until fancy,   with
all her images, is fatigued and overwhelmed,
and falls in silence and admiration at the
feet of the majestic works of God.

## OF GAME.

In an early day these prairies and wood-
lands were well filled with wild animals. The
buffalo, which once roamed over this county
in unbroken herds of countless hundreds,
were not seen here as late as 1810; but many
of their trails remain to this day.   They
would feed on Phelps and Poor Prairies, and
in the evening go to the Crab Orchard for
water; and they wore out deep paths to the
creek. One of these trails can be seen from
G. L. Owen's, and one from A. B. Scurlock's
to the creek. But  deer was here in large
droves as late as 1848, and even  yet  are
some wandering ones found. In   an early
day they were seen in great gangs, feeding
on the rich and verdant herbage that carpeted our emerald meadows.   Sometimes the
breathless stillness of the forest would  be

broke by the crack of a rifle, and hundreds
of wolves would hold their midnight carni-
val over the remains of one of these noble
animals. Bears were found in great numbers in the bottoms. Elk left in a few years
after the bison. Wildcats, raccoons, skunks,
otters, minks, ground hogs, squirrels,
opossum, rabbits, etc., are still found in
abundance. Until within a few years the
blood-shot eye of the catamount might be
seen glaring in the foliage. Serpents were
here in great profusion—copperheads, black
and blue racers, chicken, garter, green and
horn snakes, moccasins, adders, etc.; and as
an adjunct to this horrible scene were hundreds of rattle snakes. Their huge scaly
bodies could be seen shining, as they lay in
folds upon hill-sides, and when approached
would throw open their mouths in a daring
and reckless manner, giving ample warning
of their ability and disposition to defend
themselves. But they are gone, and soon
memory will lose all its wild deer. Thus
will perish forever the game which was to
our father objects of mutual pleasure and
dangers.

## OF BIRDS.

Our fathers did not find those beautiful
singing-birds here when they came that we
now have. They are creatures of civilized

countries, and follow the tide of emigration. But vultures were here, and would flop their broad wings and soar over head in great clouds when disturbed. Vast flocks of buzzards circled round and round far up in the blue ether, and made their home in the winds and clouds. Cranes, brants, wild geese, and eagles were seen, and the blue herron would stretch upward with their long, skinny necks at the sight of man. The golden oriole, blue jay, and the flaming red bird darted away among the shadowy boughs, and the lark poured his sad sweet notes on the spicy air; plovers, prairie hens, wrens, robins, ravens, crows, blackbirds, pewits, martins, thrush, quail, snipe, king-fisher, mocking-birds, pigeons, doves, yellow hammers, blue-birds are very plentiful.

There is a buzzard which sails gracefully over Northern Perçinct to which tradition ascribes a mysterious history. It was caught in a wolf-trap over forty-five years ago; and one leg still hangs down as it flies. It has been kept sight of ever since. In the same locality lives a gray eagle whose mate was shot by Dr. S. M. Mitchell over twenty-five years ago.

## OF INDIANS.

That portion of the Territory lying between the Big Muddy on the west, and the

Wabash on the east, was for over thirty years inhabited by the Shawnee tribe of Indians. And that west of Big Muddy, to the Mississippi, was occupied by the Kaskaskia Indians.

In the year 1802, a battle occurred between the two tribes. These tribes would occassionally trespass upon the hunting grounds of each other, from which quarrels ensued, and finally the battle above mentioned. It was fought by agreement on the half-way ground, in Town Mount Prairie, in the edge of Franklin county, about three miles south-west of Frankfort. The Kaskaskians were under the command of their chief John DuQuoin, then quite an old man, and a good friend to the whites. The Shawnees were commanded by a chief of a treacherous nature, which was probably the cause of the fight. As to the duration of this battle, we have no means of knowing; but the battle-ground itself, though under a high state of cultivation, can yet be located by the marks. The farms occupied by L. D. Throop and the Dennings, are at the extremes of the battle-field, the main fight taking place a little south of Mr. Throop's residence. A large number of the Shawnees were slain, and the remainder driven to the Big Muddy River, at a point about a quarter of a mile below the bridge, on the Frankfort and DuQuoin road, where, in attempting to cross they were nearly all butchered, and the tribe annihilated. The Kaskaskias after that held undisputed sway, until the encroachment of the whites drove them beyond the Mississippi.

Since the year 1802 there were a few straggling bands of hunters and fishermen in this county, but no tribe ever again claimed it. In consequence of the hostile disposition of the Indians, no white settlements were made this side of Equality until 1804, when seven brothers by the name of Jordan, John and William Browning, Joseph Estes and a man by the name of Barbrey, a brother-in-law to the Jordans, came from Smith county Tennessee, and located in Franklin county, and built a fort and block-house on the ground now occupied by the residence of Alexander McCreery.

Until 1815 little or no attempt was made by them to cultivate the soil, but they subsisted on the products of the woods. In the year 1812, James Jordan and Barbrey went out to gather wood, and they were fired on by the Indians. Barbrey was killed dead and scalped; Jordan was wounded in the legs, but was able to get to the fort. After obtaining re-inforcements from Frank Jordan's fort, they started in pursuit of the Indians and followed them as far as the Okaw

River, but did not overtake them. Barbrey
was buried at the fort, and his grave can
be seen at this day. The murder of Barbrey was but a just and inexplicable epitome
of that long catalogue of violent deaths,
ushered in by the keen crack of the savage
Indians' rifle, and ending with the hollow
thud of the murderous shot-gun in this
county.

A large portion of the Shawnee tribe
lived in Indiana, and in 1811 were camped
on the Tippecanoe, a tributary of the Wabash. The great Tecumseh was chief of the
Shawnee Indians, and at that time was preparing for war against Governor Harrison;
and while our government was    fighting
England, Tecumseh left his tribe in 1811 and
taking twelve of his warriors with him,
started south to enlist the Creek Indians to
join him. He passed through this county,
coming into it from the north-east to Marion, where he struck the Kaskaskia trail. He
followed it to the Hill place and then    on
south. About a mile south of Marion    he
was met and talked to by John Phelps, who
had been in the country but a short time
and he was frightened very badly.    But
Tecumseh was a humane Indian and was
never known to ill-treat or murder a prisoner, and denounced all who did, and employed all his authority and eloquence to

protect the helpless. In the fall he returned north, and was greatly mortified over
his brother's defeat at Tippecanoe. The next
year he was killed at the battle of the'
Thames, in Canada.

But the Shawnee Indians were not all
like Tecumseh. They were hated and dreaded
by the whites, and were overwhelmed and
obliterated by the relentless flow of the pale-
faces, and lived only in memory and history.
They once claimed this county as their own,
and the light bark canoe swam on the silver
bosom of the Saline. As they wandered
along its shores they passed forests whose
sombre depths were veiled to them by a vast
screen of drooping birch, and then they
pushed their little craft through wide-
spreading beds of water lilies, and then, entering one of Nature's solemn temples, what
weird, wonderous visions greeted their
thrilled senses! As they glided slowly along,
the heavens were almost shut out. Behind
and before them rose up trunks of trees; now
and then they stooped as they passed under
some monarch of the place. They pushed
aside the thickly trailing vines and then the
canoe would disturb a perfect surface of the
most marvelous mirror, reflecting countless
forms of leaves and twigs. How intense was
the silence, broken only by the splash of a
single blue heron, who, wondering at the

intrusion, gazed, and then spreading his great wings, rose and slowly disappeared. Such were the scenes of these dirty, greasy, filthy Indians.

Every valley of our beautiful county gives evidence of the existence of the race to which I refer. The delightful valley of the Crab-Orchard is replete with Indian history and reminiscence. But the Kaskaskias, who were friendly with the whites, continued to come to this county as late as 1828. They were sent out by Colonel Manair, a trader of Kaskaskia, to hunt for furs, etc. They would come in the fall and camp on Big Muddy, Hurricane, Crab-Orchard, Caplinger Ponds, and other streams. But these were Indians in whom the peculiar characteristics of the race had given place to some of the courtesies and confidences of civilized man. A very large number of them were camped at Bainbridge as late as 1813. James Maneece once visited this camp, and they had a large kettle of terrapins on boiling, making soup. They asked him to eat with them, but he declined. The Crain boys and others used to go to their camps on the Crab-Orchard, and have fun with them. They asked them why they did not go down on the Saline; that there was plenty of all kinds of game there; but the Indian would shake his head and say, "Griffee live there; he kill Indians." Thos. Griffee had a character for killing every Indian he could catch in the woods, and they were afraid to go down there. When they camped on Big Muddy, the white folks would go down regularly every Sunday to see them. One old Indian who came here for several years had a white wife, by the name of Ellen, said to be very handsome. He would never leave her at the camp alone on Sunday, for fear the white boys would steal her. These hunters used to go quite often to farmers' houses for something to eat.

In Northern Precinct, they got so bad that the women were afraid to stay at home alone while they were loitering around through the woods. The men banded together, and gave the Indians ten days' notice to leave the country. They produced the Governor's permit to hunt, but it was not honored. They left before the ten days were out, and were never seen in Northern Precinct again. John Roberts, the Burns and Ratcliff were in the band. Wigwams were still standing on Carl. Grave's farm, in 1820; and on Hugh Park's, as late as 1829, were traces of camps. But after 1818, they never went into the eastern part of the county. They had a camp at a spring on the farm of J. S. Neely, in 1817. Also, on Indian Camp Creek, in the Burns settlement.

A little south of the old station, near Pond
Creek, are several Indian mounds; they are
piles of dirt thrown up two feet high and
twenty feet across to set the wigwams on
to kept them dry. Many relics of the Indians
have been found in this county. On Wesley
Park's farm are rocks cut and carved in curious style by the Indians.

## OF EARLY SETTLERS.

The French settlers of Kaskaskia were
mostly engaged in fur trading, and, in pur-
suing this business, would follow up   the
streams emptying into the Mississippi, near
that place.   As no stream runs from   this
county to Kaskaskia, it is not probable that
any of these people ever entered what   is
now Williamson county until 1720.

When Renault, an agent of the Mississippi Company, left France with two hundred
miners to carry out   the mining schemes
of that company in Illinois, he bought five
hundred slaves at San Domingo, to work in
the mines. He settled at St. Phillip,   and
sent out exploring expeditions all over Illinois. He remained here twenty-four years,
and spent seven millions of dollars.   While
there is no evidence of his search in   this
county, it is almost certain that he did so.
Along the north side of Johnson county is
found a shining kind of metal resembling

—F 3

silver, and many traces of extinct mines yet remain that at some day must have been the scene of much labor and expense. To reach these mines, he would necessarily pass through this county, and if so, was the first white man ever to break its solemn silence with the tread of his foot-steps. The next probable account of white men in this county was in 1766, when four men, who had been exploring with Col. James Smith in Kentucky, crossed into Illinois at the mouth of the Tennessee, and traveled fifty miles north, where they are lost sight of forever. It is likely they were killed by the Indians in this county.

The first white men known to have been in this county was in 1796. Col. George Rogers Clarke, with one hundred and fifty men, came down the Ohio *en route* for Kaskaskia. He left Fort Massac about the 14th day of June, and marched on foot to a point seven miles north-west of Golconda. Here he turned north-west, and came into our county at the south-east corner, marched by Sarahville to Thomas Hill's place, then turned north, passed within one hundred and fifty yards of Marion on the west side, then through the east side of Phelps' Prairie to Herrin's Prairie, passing through where D. R. Harrison's fine brick mansion now stands and crossing Big Muddy at the mouth

of Pond Creek, or Odum Ford, and arrived
at Kaskaskia on the 4th day of July. This
has since been known as the Kaskaskia
Trail, and in an early day was very muddy
and hard to travel. So much so, that a new
trail, known as the "Worthen Trail," was
made through the east side of the county.
It turned north near Sarahville, and ran
along the ridge through the Hendrickson
Settlement, then into Town Mount Prairie,
and joined the old trail south-east of Du-
Quoin. In Phelps' Prairie, Clarke, suspect-
ing his Indian guides of treachery, put bayonets behind them and gave them one hour
to find the right direction or die. They
found it. Clark spent twenty days crossing
a country that at most would not have required more than four days for his sturdy
back-woodsmen to cross. From this I conclude that he built what is known as "Stone-
fort," in Saline county, near the old trail.
There are the remains of an old fort enclosing an acre of ground with dilapitated
walls of stone on three sides, and a huge
bluff on the north. A short distance from
the fort up and down stream is a block-
house. That this was built about this time
is evident from the growth of the trees in
it. It is the shape and style of those built
by white men on the frontiers. The block-
houses were built up and down the stream,

the way the Indians traveled. It is built on
a high bluff, where nearly all forts  are
built by white men. The Indians never built
any rock forts, and never entrenched  on
open, high or conspicuous places. It  was
within a short distance of the Saline River,
the regular camping ground of the Shawnee
Indians for over thirty years, who, at this
time, were at war with the whites, and mov-
ing eastward. I was unable to find and en-
graving or sculpturing on the rocks, but the
trees have been blazed and the dates grown
up. I give it as my opinion, based on  the
history of the past, that Clark built this fort.
It was occupied in 1813 by  a  family  of
Shultz's.

This brings me to the first settlement,
which occurred in 1810. Frank Jordan built
a fort in Northern Precinct. It was a stockade enclosing about one acre of land,  and
contained four log cabins and a well,  and
was about fifty yards from Pond Creek. It
is now known by the name of the "Old Station," and in 1820 half the stockade was
standing and the cabins were occupied by
James Howe and Mr. Parks. An old doctor
by the name of John Dunlap was with the
Jordans in this fort. He claimed to have been
captured by the Indians when a boy and
brought up by them to the practice of medicine. He lived a great many years and follow-

ed his profession, and always got his medicine out of the roots and herbs in the woods.

In this year three of the Dillinghams came to this county on a hunting expedition, and camped where Bazzel Holland now lives. For several years they continued to come here to hunt, and finally settled. They frequently met the Indians, but always got along friendly with them. In 1811 John Phelps settled Phelps' Prairie. Jay and McClure settled at the Odum Ford. Joseph and Thomas Griffee settled at Ward's Mill. William Donald settled the Hill place. John Manesse and his son James settled in Phelp's Prairie. During this year these settlers and some from down on Cache, built a blockhouse on the John Davis' place, west of Marion. It was built of hewed logs, and was twenty feet square, covered with slabs, and had port holes eight feet from the ground. They all went into this fort at night, and had nineteen white dogs for guards on the outside. The tracks of Indians were often seen around in the morning.

James Maneese was twenty-three years old before he knew what a doctor was. He was once sent with a note to one which he gave to a man who gave it to the doctor. Maneese thought it was a machine he was going for. But, lo, Mr. Doctor was a man! A man by the name of Hibbins settled the

west side of Herrin's Prairie during this
year, but was compelled to leave it the next.

Eighteen and twelve is memorable for the
settlement of Flanery, at Flanery Springs.
Richard Bankston settled the Spiller farm
north of Marion. An unknown hunter built
his camp on what is now Benton Russell's
farm, but he had to leave on account of the
Indians. A few more were added to Jordan's
fort, and Richard Ratcliff settled the Roberts' farm in Northern. Charles
Humphreys settled at the Stancil ford, and
commenced to keep a ferry. He built him a
small block-house, but the Indians sometimes got so bad that he had to remove his
family to Jordan's fort for safety. One night,
James Herrin, who had come out here on a
visit, stayed in the house with the ferryman.
It thundered and lightened terribly, and
they could see the Indians walking around
when it lightened. But they were all gone
before day. In 1815 Nathan Arnett settled
the Hinchliff farm, and Abraham Piatt,
William Doty and Nelson McDonald settled
near him. Solomon Snider and James Mc-
Donald moved up from Johnson county and
settled in Grassy. Dempsey Odum settled the
F. C. Kirkham farm. Aaron Youngblood settled the Jake Sanders' place. In 1816 there
were but few settlers. Joshua Tyner settled on the Eight Mile; William Lindsey the

Samuel Russell place; Jasper Crain settled on the west side of the prairie, and the next year moved to Phelps' Prairie. 1817 was more prolific of settlers. Spencer Crain settled in Phelps' Prairie. John Phelps moved to Union county. Ragsdall Rollin settled the north side of the prairie. Isaac Herrin settled the Stotlar place in Herrin's Prairie. Capt. David Springs settled the Graves' place. John Roberts bought Ratcliff's improvements. John Hooker and James Howe settled near him and Mr. Worthen. In 1818 there was a great influx of people. Phillip Russell and his three sons settled in the Eight Mile. Perkins in Herrin's Prairie. Elijah Spiller bought Bankston out. Bankston was a shrewd man, a great hunter, but a drunkard. William Burns and five brothers settled in Northern. Major Lockaleer the Burns place. George Davis the Bell place. Dickenson Garrett a little south of James Edwards. Hezekiah Garrett, the Ben Eaton farm. William Norris on Phelps' Prairie.

The settlers of 1819 were David Herring with his father-in-law, Isaac Herrin. The prairie was named after Isaac. Sion Mitchell, S. M. Mitchell and Moses Jones settled in Northern. S. M. Mitchell where he now lives. Conrad Baker in Herrin's Prairie. William and Ben Spiller in the Spiller settlement. Abraham Tippy and his son,

John, a little south of Bainbridge. Starling Hill at the Hill place, and Simpkins brothers near Hill's. 1820 is signalized by the settlement of Wadkins and his negro—the first one in the county. Dowell Russell settled the Lewis Parks place. Mark Robinson, the Kidd place. Some of the Shultz's in Saline precinct. James Stewart and his sons, on the Pease farm. 1821, David Corder settled the Erwin farm on the east, and George Davis on the west. Major James Corder settled the Stilly farm. 1822, Hamilton Corder where he now lives. Charles Erwin settled the farm on which he lived and died. Hugh Parks on the Jack Thompson place, and seven years afterwards moved where he now lives. Daniel Mosley, the Furlong place. 1823, William Campbell settled Blairsville, and Sam. Stacks Southern Precinct.

I have now given all the settlers up to 1822. These I have denominated "the early settlers," for three reasons: First, it gives us a settlement in all the precincts of the county, and Second, they produced no change in the country—neither improving it nor destroying the game, but lived like the Indians, mostly in the woods. Third, the influx of immigration swelled into such a stream that it would be impossible to keep trace of individual settlers with anything like accuracy. The Bowles, Lewis, Wrights, Ar-

nolds, Hunters, Phimesters, Bakers and Tur-
ners, all settled in early days.

The settlement of Marion deserves    a
notice. Poor Prairie, by William Benson in
1826. He built a cabin where the Cox place
is.  Soon after this, Martin Spiller settled
the Goddard place, and Tipo S. Williams
the Aikman place, and Mr. Tyner built  a
cabin where the C. & S. R. R. depot now
stands.  In 1835, Benson bought Tyner's improvements, which extended over the present site of Marion, and he built a cabin
where the widow of Col. James D. Pully now
lives.  At that time a cabin was standing
where Young & Kern's store now stands, in
a decayed condition, and no one knew anything of it.  Benson kept hotel, and his house
was used as a court-house for a while.  He
cultivated corn and wheat where the square
was laid out.  Silas Grattan settled the Barham place. James McCoy, the Stockton place.
Jacob Goodall settled on the  Goodall  farm
southeast of Marion in 1828.  I will now pro-
ceed to give a description of the character,
manners, etc., of our fathers, and first of

## THEIR CHARACTER.

I have tried, though with conscious  im-
perfection to describe the country our first
settlers found when they came here. It was
this lovely country, with its still past, and

glorious future, that awakened a feeling of
independence and spirit of enterprise among
the settlers. They were generally the humb-
ler class from Tennessee, Kentucky,
North and South Carolina; but there is
scarcely a state in the Union that has not
furnished us some immigrants, and there is
no country where more singular, more eccen-
tric, more opposite characters were found.
Here was the brave, the passionate, the generous, the sincere, the fickle, the bold, the
modest, the devout, and the wicked. Here
were some devoid of treachery and malice,
others vindictive and penurious. Some were
promoters of education, and some were idl-
ers. Here were the melancholy and the
happy. They were very credulous and believed nearly everything they heard, no matter how exaggerated, and hence imposition
and misfortune was often their lot. They
came here big with enterprise, elated with
hope, full of their own abilities. They trust-
ed to themselves for life. They were poor,
but of unmixed blood. There were no half-
breeds, neither of Indians nor other obnoxious races. In private life they lived
with republican austerity, and in society
moved with chivalrous spirit. They settled
on the margins of the little prairies, on the
banks of streams, and near large springs.
They built cabins out of round logs, which

they chinked and daubed to keep out the
winter's cold and summer's heat. The door
was hung with cypress vines, and the yard
was decorated with sun-flowers, hollyhocks
and poseys, showing that woman, under all
circumstances, has something sweet and noble in her life. Many of these cabins are
still standing, and there are none of us, if
our ancestors were traced back a few genera-
tions, but would find them in one of these
cabins, where the midnight wolves howled
their nightly serenade. It was in one of
these rude structures, surrounded by an unbroken forest, that the author of this volume, still an humble boy, was cast out upon
the cold charities of an unfeeling and incon-
stant world, to live in a sinful day and suffer
the destinies of men. And these old woods
are still eloquent with the reminiscences of
long ago—not the stuff that dreams are
made of, but the rank charms and rich loves
of the past, loading the vehicle of memory
and oppressing the soul.

Two-thirds of the early settlers followed
the occupation of hunting. They cultivated
small patches of corn for bread. The other
third followed farming. While eight acres
was a large farm, they made good livings
and had something to give their children.
Besides these two classes, there was a va-
grant class that sprung up in the last forty

years, who roamed through the woods un-
influenced by attachment and unfettered by
principle, stealing hogs and sheep. But they
have all disappeared. The settlers lived
calm, quiet lives, remote from the active
bustle of more civilized life. Their sur-
roundings imparted to them generous feelings, gentle manners and a language of
liquid softness. Hospitality with them was
a part of human nature, and not a religious
rite. They were as generous as their soil was
productive. Nature had bestowed food upon them with a liberal hand, and taught them
to share it with the hungry. Social intercourse was more general than now, more
hearty, less formal, and more valued. Friendships were warmer and deeper. When a man
got sick, his neighbors would go break his
ground, plant his crop and cultivate it for
him. And it was thought no hardship to
ride fifteen miles for this purpose, or even
visiting as friends. The world has not exhibited an example of a more happy race
than our early settlers. Their kindness was
bounded only by their capacity. Nothing
that a neighbor wanted was too good for
him to borrow. While some of them had
vices of savages, most of them had the virtues of men. They were true to their country, true to their friends, their homes and
their God. They hardly ever forgave an in-

sult or forgot a kind act; and if their vengeance was terrible, their generosity was
great.  Their lives may seem to us hard,
lonesome and wearied by lifeless monotony;
but they were passed happily.  Some of our
old men have told me their young days were
the best and sweetest part of life. They heard
the same song-birds that we hear.  Their
faces were fanned by the same breeze; but
they were surrounded by the rich influence
of wild, untamed Nature.  Cowardice was a
foreigner.  They were thoughtful,    grave-
looking set of men, with long beards, and
generally had but little to say.  But the grav-
ity of the stock has been changed by grafts
from without, and these early characteristics
are observable now only in our oldest men.
They live in the past, and only look to the
future with gratitude and hope to see their
children fairly gain wealth and honor in a
day of culture and  refinement.  Some  of
these old men live in cabins with but  little
around them, and it is no index to the position they once held, or the influence  they
exerted, to see them living that way now.
They might have been captains in the militia, or served as judge, sheriff, etc., in the
county.  Mr. O. West, once a captain in the
Army, now lives in a humble cottage. General John Davis lived on a farm in  a  log
house.  These men never resorted to slan-

der; when they spoke of a man their language clearly showed no malice. They were generous to faults, and honest in their dealings. The children of those who followed faming are our best livers. The Herrings, Parks, Russells, Davis, Roberts, Stewarts, Arnolds, were not hunters, and their children are our wealthiest farmers. Those who followed hunting are now generally poor.

But our fathers had many hardships to lessen the joys of life. They were often without the necessities of life. They had but few store goods, and had to go to Equality for salt, to Shawneetown for groceries and domestics. They had but few horses, and most of the traveling was done on foot. Even in a very late day, they would go to mill, carrying two bushels of corn on their shoulders. But, happily for our people, none need have such hardships now. Our mothers were among the border beauties of the Great West. They were very plain, untrammeled by stages and ceremonies. They did not have white hands, nor willow waists, and consequently had coarse, awkward, brawny health. Still, in this wilderness, they had much of their refinement belonging to their sex. They had something about them that was womanly and attractive. They did not swear, do, nor say anything that was sug-

gestive of immorality. They associated with
men, and very coarse ones, and were intimately acquainted with all their affairs.
They were accustomed to the woods and
dangers, and learned to be strong of hand
and nerve, and to keep cool. They would
fight as quick as the men, and many of them
were excellent shots and could shoot a deer
or turkey as well as bake a hoe-cake. Their
necks were sun-burnt, and their hair hung
down or was twisted in a little knot on the
back of the head. They wore no ruffles,
bias stripes or flounces, but had a comliness
of their own. It was not the paltry pretti-
ness of gait nor manners that lent beauty to
their frontier charms, but it was stalwart,
untrained grace that made them models of
beauty. Their ringlets fell in troublesome
abundance and would not be confined. Their
cheeks, if they could but know the absence
of sunbeam caresses and the boisterous
kisses of the wind, would show the clearest
marble-white and bonniest bloom. They shuf-
fled their limbs slip-shod along trails in
search of animals, and of whose sound
strength the owner had but little thought.
They had arms which split wood and carried water; whose whiteness and mould
would fit them rather for the adornment of
golden clasps and folds of ancient lace. Their
houses were neat and tasty. They had no

fine furniture, no bright, baize carpet covered the floor; but in the yard a stump  or
box contained forest flowers; luxuriant
branches of evergreens hung in the corners,
and festoons of oak leaves and cypress vines
covered the whitewashed walls of the house;
and panseys, ferns and pinks fringed the
walks.

Many of our older ladies look back with
tears in their eyes on these fair dwellings.
How bright are the scenes, and how sacred
are the joys which surround them! Memory
wraps a halo of beauty, peace and glory
around them, and binds anew their charms
to the heart. Little did they care for the
smiles of the gay world of fashion that glitter and gleam on the paths of modern belles.
While our fathers  preached, commanded,
hunted and plowed, our mothers spun, wove,
cultivated flowers, and exerted every gentle,
womanly influence. If a woman wounded
the feelings of her neighbor, and a recon-
ciliation had to be effected, some little chord,
buried deep under the accumulated debris
of pride, indifference and wounded vanity,
was struck by a sympathetic hand, and
thrilled and quivered into perfect harmony.
These little, impulsive acts were genuine in-
spirations. Many a man has been led to
the fold of friendship, and many a woman's
life has been strengthened by the sponta-

neous infusion of sympathetic feelings. They loved their husbands, brothers and sons, and were as ready to join them in their sports and amusements, as to share their privations and dangers. They provided lolly-pops for school-girls, and ginger-cakes for boys, and flying mares and swings for festive days. I have asked our old ladies what hardships they had to encounter in the early settlement of this county; but they gave so many and varied accounts, that it was hard to generalize their troubles. They were often left alone, surrounded by wild animals and were subject to frequent hardships. I will relate one scene which I saw when a boy, illustrative of those early days. It was one of the hardest scenes that it is the allotment of men to meet. It was a handsome young woman, sitting on a plowbeam, nursing her baby. She had just been plowing, and had taken her babe up from its grassy bed, and sat down to rest. This was a hard sight. New feelings sprang up slowly in my heart, and I could hardly keep my countenance from arguing humanity by sighs and sobs. This lovely woman met Fate's stern demand with a brave patience that was truly grand and heroic. The birds had learned to love her, and as the transparent clouds drifted like currents and

—F 4

waves of gauze athwart the sky, they whis-
tled their cheerful lullabies of sympathy and
encouragement to her. But she was a
widow, and afterwards married happy, and
Williamson County has not since been tar-
nished by a scene like this, which must
wither the pride and bring a blush of shame
to the cheek of every person who has the
least spark of humanity in his bosom. If it
is objected that this incident is not worthy
of historic mention, I will answer that the
hardships of our people are a part of my
subject, and my heart is full of it.

But few of the early settlers are now
living. Since we have parted from them,
winter has come and gone, spring has glad-
dened us with beauty, blossoms and fruits.
And the summer of life is now pouring in
profusion into the lap of our destiny the
highest privileges of civilized man, to be
gathered and garnered for our comfort.
Much of the real character of our people
remains unchanged, and this county today,
contains a bold, brave, generous class of
citizens, distinguished for intelligence, honesty and high moral culture. They are a
people which will compare favorably, in
those virtues and graces with ennoble character and render life happy, with those of
any part of the Great West.

## OF DRESS.

Among the men there were two styles of dressing worn—one by those who followed farming, and one by those who were hunters. The hunters, who were by far the largest class, wore a hunting-shirt, which was a large linsey or domestic gown, open before and fastened with a belt, and reached below the knees. Under this was a pair of domestic pants, a common vest, and deerskin moccasins on their feet, and a deer or a coon skin cap on their heads. This was the dress, both winter and summer, and in this garb, the hunter might be seen wading the snow of winter, or crushing the flowers of summer. At church and public gatherings, the bloodiest man was generally considered the best dressed.

The dress of the farmers was a little different. In place of the hunting-shirt, they had a sack-coat, made of linsey. In place of domestic pants, they generally wore dressed buck skin, and in place of the cap, they had the palmetto hat. The dressing of the women was still more odd and singular. They raised their own cotton and flax, spun and wove them into such garments as they needed. Six yards was considered an extravagant amount to put into one dress, which was made plain, with two widths in the skirt, the front one cut gored. The waist was up under their arms, with a draw string between the shoulders behind. The sleeves were made very large, and tapered to the wrist, and the most fashionable had these sleeves filled with a kind of pad which made them look like a bolster, and were called "sheep shank sleeves." Those who could afford it, used feathers, which gave the sleeve the appearance of an inverted balloon from the elbow up, and were called "pillow sleeves." Some of these were so large that they almost shut out the face from view, and extended up to their ears. Papers were used in absence of pads and feathers. Graceless young rascals would speak of kissing the girls at parties as "squeezing the pillows." The bonnet was a tow bonnet, made of splits; but the most fashionable wore Leghorn hats, with the brim about ten inches wide, tied up with a ribbon in a bow-knot on top. They wore a great many ribbons and bows, but no jewelry. If a girl could succeed in getting a little indigo blue in her tow dress, she was considered as "putting on airs."

The tow dress was superseded by the cotton dress. Their petticoats and bed gowns were made of linsey, and a small copperas handkerchief filled the place around the neck now occupied by a gorgeous ring of ruffles. They went barefooted in sum-

mer. In winter they wore moccasins and
shoe packs. A very nice thing compared
with the elegant Morocco slipper, embossed
with bullion, worn now by their grand-
daughters. In going to church they would
carry their shoes in sight, and then stop and
put them on. The coats of the women and
the hunting shirts of the men were hung upon wooden pegs around the walls of the
cabin, and one could see their stock in this
line at a glance. They had none of the ruffles, silk hats, curls, combs, rings and jewels that adorn and beautify our belles. Many
of them were grown before they ever saw
inside of a store, or even knew that there
was such a thing. Instead of the toilet, they
handled the wheel and shuttle. Instead of
the piano and guitar, the sickle and weeding
hoe. Instead of challis and silk, they were
contented with their linsey and copperas-
colored tow for dresses, and to cover their
heads with bonnets made with five-hundred
cotton yard. And in this severe simplicity
they lived and were happy. Their hearts
pulsed in responsive beats to each other's
woes and were borne on the same wave of
joy. Reared in simplicity, surrounded by
poverty, cared for by brave parents, their
lives were one long dream of sunshine, unbroken by a single storm-cloud poured out

as a shameful libation to dim the horizon of their happiness.

In 1840, the styles which I have described were nearly all gone, and those of the present day took their place. The gray moss-covered rocks, the aged oak, the green thicket the emerald prairies are all unchanged. Nature's usual robes remain the same. Man is the only thing in Nature that changes the styles of its covering. Probably because originally made to live without clothes, and God placed them on him because of his sin, and man, finding himself in an unnatural condition, has ever been hard to please.

## OF FURNITURE.

Coming here as the early settlers did in wagons, over execrable roads, they could bring no furniture with them, and, consequently they had nothing but what they made, which was rude enough. Their bedsteads consisted of a fork drove in the ground and poles laid in it; then into the walls of the cabin. This was covered with boards, and these with straw, deer or bear skins. The tables were made of boards pegged on to a frame with four legs crossing each other in the center like a saw-buck. The furniture for the table for several years consisted of a few pewter dishes, plates and spoons, but mostly of wooden bowls, trenchers and noggins. If these were not to be had, gourds and hard-shelled squashes were used. Some few people used the delft ware, but it was considered of no account by many, as it was easily broken—and then it dulled their scalping and clasp knives. Tea ware was too small for men, but was good enough for women and children. Iron pots, knives and forks were brought here when the people came. Deer skins, stretched over a hoop, and perforated with a hot wire were used as a sifter, and almost every house had a loom, and every woman was a weaver.

But this rude and noisy furniture has given place to sewing machines, rose-wood pianos, organs, and marble tables, which are now frequently met with. All kinds of edge tools were scarce and very valuable in an early day. So it was a long time before the carpenters improved on the furniture. In 1840, at least two turning lathes were put up in the county, and they made some round bed posts, which were long enough for flag poles.

## OF DIET.

For a while after our fathers came here, they had some of the provisions which they brought with them; but soon they were cut off from all supplies but those which Na-

ture had placed within their reach, and such
as they made by their own exertions.  If
the furniture for the table was rude,  the
articles of diet corresponded with it.  Wild
meats were plentiful.  Small patches of corn
were raised, which, being beaten in a mortar, made good bread, but they could  not
shut their teeth close on account of the grit
in the bread.  Hog and hominy was a favorite dish, as was also hoecake and gravy.
Johnny cakes and pones were staples  for
breakfast and dinner—milk and mush were
used for supper.  Fish, of  course,  were
abundant.  All kinds of  greens,  such  as
dock, and polk, were eaten.  Roasting-ears,
pumpkins, beans, squashes  and  potatoes
were raised  in "truck patches," and used
by all.  The pot-pie was the standard dish
for log-rollings and house raisings.  Coffee
and tea were not much used in an early day
—they were thought to be slops that would
not "stick to the ribs."  The genuine  back-
woodsman would say that they were good
for sick women and children.  They were
surrounded by all kinds of wild fruits, such
as grapes, cherries, plums, paw-paws,  per-
simmons, crabapples, red and  black haws,
and berries.  These  fruits  still  grow  in
great abundance in this county.  There were
both  butchers  and  cooks,  and  had  no
"Bridgets" or waiting-girls.  With refine-

ment and culture, came that knowledge
which has produced that variety of diet
which makes the Americans the most independent people on earth.

## OF MORALS.

For a long time in the early history of
our county, there was neither law nor gospel, but there was a set of moral maxims
which answered the place of law. Everybody understood what was right, and the
man who did not do this was looked down
upon. For instance, it was a duty for every man to help fight the Indians, or help
raise houses; if he refused, he need not
ask men to help him. No man was allowed
to draw a deadly weapon in a fight, and if
he did, everybody was against him. They
had an innate or hereditary detestation of
the crime of theft, and any person caught
stealing was generally doomed to carry the
"United States Flag on his back," to-wit:
thirteen stripes. Bastardy was an offense
of rare occurrence, the chivalrous temper of
the people was so great that the guilty auth-
or was in great danger of personal violence
from the brothers and father of the girl.
Family honor was then esteemed very highly. People in those days had a great deal of
veracity, and such a thing as perjury was
unknown, until that unprincipled class of

citizens which I mentioned elsewhere, sprang
up in the county. Generally, they esteemed
their word as good as their bond. The hunting class, as the game began to get scarce,
were mostly idle and unoccupied, and the
idleness tempted to dissipation, and hence
whisky shops gained a footing in the county
as early as 1835, followed by shooting
matches, gander pullings and horse races,
which were the schools in which their ap-
petites were trained and nursed into mischief. When intemperance had extended its
ravages, profanity overspread the country,
which before was unknown. Licentiousness
was uncommon among the early settler, but
is now practiced to an alarming extent. This
is caused by the countenance given by the
public to those men who lave in the lecher-
ous sea of prostitution.

### OF HUNTING.

From 1810 to 1835, two-thirds of our
fathers followed hunting for a living, and,
consequently they never made anything; but
those who stuck to the farms are the wealthy
ones now. The hunters cared but little for
worldly honors and distinction, and scarcely
ever looked to the future. These rangers
of the woods were a hardy race, accustomed
to labor and privation. Their forms were
developed to the fullest vigor; many of them
idled away their aimless lives on the fertile

plains that lay untilled before them, following some phantom that glowed with a treacherous gleam into scenes that were as false as their pleasures were hollow.

Early hunters were more like the primitive savage than any other men. Their habits and characters assumed a cast of simplicity mingled with ferocity, taking their colorings from the scenery and objects about them, with no companion but Nature and the rifle. By natural instinct they were ever alive to guard against danger, and provide food. Great observers of nature, they rivaled the beast of prey in discovering the haunts of game and their habits. Callous to the feelings of danger, by constant exposure they feared nothing. Of law they knew but little; their wish was law, and to obtain this they did not scruple at the means or cost; but these strong, active honest backwoodsmen were firm friends and generous men. Some of them still live among us; the most prominent are Hamilton Corder, James Maneece, Samuel Russell and William Chitty. But that bold race of which they are specimens, is fast passing away. If I was not a criminal I would go to them for relief, but if I was a criminal I would shun their eyes. These old men love to retreat to the forest and there relate their hunting scrapes. They were daring experts; not a hole in the county but has been ransacked by these hardy men.

They knew every rock, stream, lake, shoal and valley in the county. They have dropped their hooks into every stream, and set their traps in every drift, and bayou. All kinds of game abounded in the woods, and all kind of fish flashed their silver scales in the sun on the bosom of our waters. They were conversant with the character of every animal, fish and bird in the country. The regular hunter would start out about an hour by sun, bending his course towards the setting sun, over undulating hills, under the shade of large forest trees, beautifully festooned with grape vines and dark deep moss; wading through rank weeds and grass, now viewing some winding creek doubtful of its course, and of his own, his restless eye caught everything around. The guard of his own safety, relying on himself for protection, and at every step the strong passions of hope and fear called into exercise, he sought ominous presages of good or bad luck in everything around. The croakings of the raven and the howl of the wolf were signs. A turned leaf or a blade of grass pressed down, the uneasiness of wild animals, flight of birds were all paragraphs to him. These men needed fortitude to sustain their reflections. They felt the pangs which solitude

gives, and had heaven the sigh which affection prompted.  Beset by dangers, despond-
ency stood ready to seize their souls. Sometimes they would go where there was an is-
land of foliage on the prairie, standing  out
of the low billows of prairie grass that serg-
ed away till the feathery tufts broke like
foam against the circles of the horizon, and
their eagle eyes swept around the country
for game.  Sometimes they would go to
green thickets, whose solitary loneness was
awful; here they would see the wolf stealing through the  gloom  aud  snuffing  the
scent of the intruder; and now and then the
blood-shot  eye  of  the catamount  glare
through the foliage.   Wolves were so common as to become a public nuisance, and after a reward of one dollar a scalp was offered for their scalps, several men followed
the business of killing  them  for a living.
They had dogs trained to jump the wolf and
then run backward, the wolf following to
where the hunter lay concealed.  Among the
most noted wolf hunters were Gideon Alexander, Parson Crouch, William Chitty and
Jesse  Childers.  They averaged about fifteen wolves a day.  In storms, the ravens
were seen winging their way to cover; the
bench-legged coyote quickly trotted to his
hole; the piercing cry of the wolf was borne
upon the winds, but the fearless hunter was

not disturbed for then he was sure of
game. Deer licks and turkey pens were a common thing until a recent day. The hunting of
wild bees, which existed here in countless
millions, was a daily business. Bear hunting was a dangerous but interesting amusement, and continued as late as 1845.

## OF SPORTS.

Our fathers indulged in many rude ath-
letic sports, which have long since given
place to the more refined amusements of
our day. As long as a higher value was set
on physical endowments than on mental,
these rude sports were continued. Prominent among them was horse-racing. This
'was carried on mostly in the west half of
the county, and was often the scene of bloodshed and much confusion. Our people have
not entirely outgrown it yet. From 1820 to
1830, and occasionally since, the barbarous
practice of gander-pullings was carried on.
It was regularly kept up at Josiah Dillard's
and Solomon Snider's, at Christmas and at
all large gatherings. The way they were
conducted was shameful in the extreme.
Plenty of whisky was first provided, then a
ponypurse was made up, or a premium offered. A gander was next taken and his
neck thoroughly soaped, when he was tied
by the legs to a springing-pole, head downward, eight or nine feet from the ground;

the riders then mounted and went at full speed; one man stood under the gander with a whip to keep the horses going. The first man who got hold of the gander generally turned the feathers the wrong way and made neck sleeker than ever. The gander would flap his wings and squall for life, when an expert rider got hold of him, in such a manner as to make the blood grow cold. Sometimes a greedy fellow would hold on until his horse ran from under him, and then he would generally strike the ground with that portion of his body which, in stooping posture, is the fairest mark for assault. Running, jumping and wrestling were the common amusements at neighborhood gatherings, and the best wrestler and fastest runner were men of notoriety. Every boy had his bow and arrow, and spent a great part of his time in the woods. Skill in shooting with the bow was a great virtue. The hunters learned to imitate the cry of all kinds of animals, and the whistle of all kinds of birds. To bleat like a fawn, howl like a wolf or gobble like a turkey, were accomplishments common among all. They had learned it from the Indians. Dancing was a favorite amusement with the people of the west side of the county. Those on the east side were not noted for sports of any kind, but were better hunters. At all weddings and house-

raisings they had a dance, and people would
come twenty-five miles to them.  They knew
nothing of the waltz, schottische  or  polka
of our day; but the "Irish Trot," three and
four-handed reels and jigs  were  tramped
out  to  perfection.  Cottonpickings  were
common in an early day, and they were followed by a "play," where  the  boys  would
kiss the girls from "Julius Cæsar"  to  the
Fourth of July."  It was not dishonorable,
because it brought no bashful blush to trip
down the girls' cheeks in stipple dots; but
the sweet, love-pressed smile baptized her
lips, and sent an electric  radiation  which
caught up his heart and made it  dance  a
polka in his mouth.  Cards, dice and other
such gambling instruments, were wholly unknown among the early settlers; but from
1835 to 1870, were used by a large number
of our people.  Now  there  are  but  few
gamblers in the county.  Singings were of
frequent occurence until within a few years.
Fox-chases, the pride of every  sportsman,
are  still enjoyed in this county.  General
hunts,with fifty on a side,  were  practiced
twenty-five years ago.  They would march
through the woods to a common rendezvous,
and have a barbecue.

## OF WEDDINGS.

The early inhabitants of this county generally married young.  There was no distinc-

tion in rank or class, and hence, no fetters
on alliances. The whole neighborhood was
on hand at a wedding, for it was sure to be
followed by a dance or frolic; and that too,
without the labor of building a cabin or
planing a scout. The weddings in this county were conducted in other respects the same
at this day, with the exception of the time.
They were then always celebrated just before dinner, and the parties were dressed in
home-made clothes, and the bride wore
buck-skin gloves. The chase after "Black
Betty," so common in the West in an early
day, was never practiced here. After the
wedding, the infare was celebrated, then a
log cabin was erected by the neighbors for
the young couple.

The young people went out, one by one,
from the happy circles of their fathers, ex-
changing a place beneath the old roof for a
new and untried one out in the wild world.
To them it was the balmy time of life. Hope
carpeted the future with flowers; all was
bright by the anticipated joy of the future.
They were our fathers and mothers. Some
of them have realized their fondest hopes
and brightest dreams, amid the storms that
have swept along the tracks of life. Others
who have battled long in winters' cold and
summers' heat, have ever had the ghastly

—F 5

spectre of poverty at their sides, pointing
to a destiny of wretchedness and dispair,
while the sunny side of life was in view.
Divorce was never heard of among the first
settlers of this county, but as the practice
of marrying has been kept up in a more sinful day, the practice of obtaining divorces
has also grown up, until now, it is spoken
of as a small and un-noticeable event.

## WORKINGS.

Workings were the result of the condition of the country. In counties where they
build frame , brick or adobe houses, no considerable number of hands are necessary,
but in the forest, where they raise log houses
it requires a large number. So, on the
prairies, where there are no logs to roll, these
workings are not known; but where the
farms are cut out of the wilderness, the
farmer needs the aid of his neighbors to
roll the heavy logs together. Then the
workings were those of planing scouts, cam-
paigns, raising log cabins, which were followed by log-rollings, wood-choppings, rail-
splittings and corn-shuckings. At these
gatherings they always had a good time.
Whiskey was provided, or no work done certain. These workings were attended by all
the neighbors, and are kept up unto this
day; and have always been a source of fun,

amusement and mutual benefit to our people.

## SLAVERY.

Illinois Territory was a slave Territory, and contained several hundred slaves; but the Constitution of 1818 prohibited slavery within the State; and provided for the manumition of the slaves. Most of the citizens of this county were from the South; but few of them brought slaves with them. Wadkins brought a negro with him, which he always called free, and Frank Jordan had two negro slaves, and the excitement on the question of slavery ran very high until 1818. The negroes were sometimes kidnapped and taken South, and sold, and sometimes taken East and freed. When the state was admitted, almost all the negroes were taken to Missouri and sold. When the question of slavery was settled beyond controversy, some of the negroes were brought back and freed, as provided by law. Alexander McCreery went to Missouri and brought back an old negress slave that his father had owned. He also bought her husband, Richard Inge, out of slavery for $300, and settled them upon eighty acres of land which, by frugality, they finally paid for, and are now living on, in the northeast part of this county. Four miles southeast of Marion, the Ellis' settled in an early day. They lived quietly and raised large families. These, and a few negroes in the northeast corner of the county, were all the negroes in the county until after the war, when a few families settled near Marion. It was a presumption of law that all negroes were slaves, and hence they could not settle in this county without providing their freedom. About the year 1857, a negro girl, living near Marion, was kidnapped by a band of ruffians, who started South with her to sell her into bondage; but such a thing was too grating to the souls of our people. The hue and cry was levied, and she was rescued from the life of a helpless, toiling slave, and restored to that liberty and freedom which God gave to all nature.

## CHURCHES.

The first church built in this county was called "Squat," and was located on what is now the farm of Thomas Sanders, in the year 1819. It is now greatly decayed, but enough remains to show that it was a house. The next church was "Rich Grove" built on Herrin's Prairie, in 1820. It was a regular Baptist church, and Isaac Herrin was its first and almost only preacher. In 1823, the Davis, Corders and Parks built a log church, a little north of where James Mayes now lives. They were Baptists, but had no minister, only as Charles Led, the celebrated witch master, would ride down from Hamilton County. In 1824 the Methodists put up a church in Northern. The Burns boys were good howlers, and they did the principal part of the work. Six years afterward it was burned down. The first church on the Eight Mile was erected near Samuel Russell, in 1836. "Gum Spring" Church, in Saline, was built soon after. The "Old Sweet Gum" was built in Marion in 1847. It was a Baptist church, and was soon followed by a Presbyterian church. There are now four large churches in Marion: A Baptist, a Christian, and two Methodists, and the county is well supplied with churches in every part. The churches in an early day had but few members, but they were very pious. Our fathers had their first meetings in their cabins, but as the county began to be settled up, and as early as 1835, they held campmeetings in the groves, the only temples built by God himself, and, therefore, the only ones worthy of Him; for there the beauties of nature taught them gratitude and adoration towards Him, whom the universe worships. The religion of those days was more practical than theoretical. They did not spend their time in cavilings about "isms" or ordinances, but went quietly along, accepting the doctrine as preached, adored their God, cherished their kind, served their friends and country, and lived in their lives that religion, engraven on the heart of the author of these words. This was the religion of our first parents. It is yours. It is mine. It is the religion of all ages and all people. Sages have never ceased to worship in silence this religion. While fanatics and fools have tinged the earth with blood of men by discussions and religious disputes, they have laid aside systems and applied themselves to doing good, the only road to happiness. The preachers claimed to hold their commission to preach from God, who had given them tongues to adore Him, and hands to help in their race, and hence they were listened to as men "having authority." The early piety and simple faith of our fathers have not been duplicated by our generation, partly because many ministers have sprung up who, if they were called to preach at all,either entered upon the work before the time, or are wholly unfit to preach for the want of sense, education or other qualifications; and partly on account of the change in our life which has unfettered the mind of many, and caused them to throw off the dogmas and superstitions of early days, such as witchcraft, etc., and assume a station above the vale of serfdom, far upon the plains of common sense.

Though these men were plain, unassuming and firm believers in religion, the keen crack of a rifle on Sunday was neither offensive or unusual. They generally went to church with their dogs and guns, and perhaps killed a deer on the way. And as I have said, the bloodiest man was the best dressed. They carried their guns to church partly for protection, and partly to provide food for dinner. The camp-meetings were held in the fall, and lasted for two or four weeks. The entire family took their beds and provisions, and moved into log camps erected near the "shed," which was a large roof set on high posts, and the floor was covered with straw. They always had a good time at these meetings, and could be heard for a great distance singing and praising God. Most every pious person shouted in those days; none were afraid to shout. It was a grand and solemn scene; away at midnight some one would get religion, and the shouting break out anew, and hundreds of people might be seen in every conceivable stage of excitement, some down by saplings, some on their knees, some running, jumping and hallooing at the top of their voices, and all giving vent to sundry expletives of praise and adoration. Such was the effect of this early pulpit orator that none could long resist their stir-

ring appeals, and the terrible doom which
they pronounced against the ungodly. But
these early hallucinations have rapidly
passed away, and will soon be numbered
among the things that were.    The faith in
Christ still remains firm and unalterable,
but the more boisterous and noisy devotion-
al exercises are heard and seen only in a
few places.    That religion which was    the
hope   and   consolation   of   our fathers is
passing away, and cold, constrained, phleg-
matic formalism taking its place too   much.
The churches of this county are many and
prosperous, and have exerted an influence
in subordinating   wickedness,   encouraging
education and morality.   But I met   some
old men who told me that in the early day,
when they neither had gospel nor meetings
that the people were peaceable, friendly and
happy; and as soon as preachers came into
the country they got up "isms," "sects" and
"systems," which ended in jars   and   feuds
among the people, and that they have never
seen any peace since.   A diversity of opinion
engenders strife and ill will, and these de-
story peace.   A genuine system of religion
ought not to produce a diversity of opinion.

## OF MILLS.

The first machinery used by our   fathers
for making meal, was the hominy block or

mortar. It was made of a large block of wood, three feet long, with an excavation burned in one end, wide at the top, and narrow at the bottom, so that the action of the pestle on the bottom threw the corn up the sides, from which it continually fell to the center. When the corn was soft, the mortar did very well for making meal, but was slow work when it was hard. They sometimes used a sweep of springing, elastic wood, thirty feet long, to lessen the toils of pounding the grain. When the corn was too soft to be beaten, a still more simple machine than the mortar was used. It was the grater, a half circular piece of tin, perforated with a punch from the concave side, and nailed by its edges to a block of wood, when the ear of corn was rubbed on the rough edges of the holes, and the meal fell through on a board and was discharged into a bowl. The mortar has not been used in this county since 1827; but the grater was used as late as 1855. Hand mills came into use about 1820, and were better than the grater or mortar. They were made of two circular stones, placed in a hoop, and a staff was let into a hole in the upper runner, near the outer edge and the upper end, through a hole in a board fastened to the joist. Two persons could work at it at once. The grain was put in by hand. These mills are still in use in Palestine. It was a mill of this kind that Jesus Christ alluded to when, in speaking of the destruction of Jerusalem, he said: "Two women shall be grinding at a mill; the one shall be taken and the other left." The first horse-mill built in this county was built by Ragsdale Rollins, in 1817, on the north side of Phelps' Prairie. It was a new thing, and people went a long way to see it. In 1822, Solomon Snider removed it to the west side of Eight Mile. William Burns built the next one in 1819, in the Burns' Settlement. He also, in the same year, put up the first cotton-gin in the county.

The next cotton-gin was put up by Jonathan Herrin, on the Dilliard farm in 1825. At this time they used to go to "Harmony Town" Indiana, for carding. Delilah Harrison, mother of D. R. Harrison, remembers this occurrence well. About that time the Burnes put up their mill, Martin Duncan built one on the north edge of Phelp's Prairie. Burnes had improved his mill so that by 1830 he could grind twenty-five bushels of corn a day, and his boys would take meal on horse back to Equality, forty miles, and swap it for salt. In 1823 John Roberts put up a horse mill on his farm. In 1823 John Lamb built a mill on Herrin's Prairie, which was afterwards removed by Jasper Crain to Phelp's Prairie. About the

year 1825, George Davis put up a mill on
the Erwin farm, and in a few years Stephen
Stilly built one at his residence. Soon after
this McDonald built the first water or tub
mill, on the Saline in the Tanner settlement.
The next was built by George Davis. Seven
years later, John Davis built the third, now
known as the Sims mill. Still later, Stephen
Blair put up a water mill on Big Muddy. In
1838 William Ryburn built a good horse-
mill on the Eight Mile, and Yost built one in
Marion. The first steam-mill was built by
Milton Mulkey in Marion in 1845. The next
by Erwin and Furlong, in 1856, at Crab
Orchard. In 1862 Herrins, Polk and Harrison
built the Herrin Prairie mill. In 1870, Mann
and Edward built a large woolen manufac-
tory. Now the county is well supplied with
both saw and flouring mills.

## OF PESTILENCE.

This county has suffered less from pes-
tilence, failures and drouth than any county
in the state. The seasons are good, and people generally healthy. The doctor bills for
the entire county do not exceed $40,000 a
year. The cholera made its first appearance in July 1849, but caused only a few
deaths. It re-appeared in 1866, and lasted
for six weeks, during which over twenty-
five persons were taken away, and the city

of Marion vacated. Among the deceased were the three beautiful Ferguson girls, ladies without parallel in all the arena of beauty and refinement. The small-pox has visited this county on several occasions, but never resulting in many deaths until 1873, when a good many died in the south side of the county. The mortality rate in this county, on a basis of population of 23,000 is three per cent.

## OF WITCHES.

The belief in witchcraft prevailed to a great extent in the east side of this county in an early day. To the witch was ascribed the usual powers of inflicting strange diseases destroying cattle by shooting them with a ball of hair, and inflicting curses and spells on guns. More ample powers for mischief can not be imagined. The means by which the witch inflicted these diseases were one of the hidden mysteries which no one but the witch understood; and no wonder, for there never existed any such power on earth.

The way they got to be witches was by drawing their own blood, writing their own names in it, and giving it to the devil, thus making a league with him. From 1818 to 1835, there were a great many witches in this county. The most noted one was an old lady by the name of Eva Locker, who lived

on Davis' prairie.  She could do wonders,
and inflict horrible spells  on the  young,
such as fits, twitches, jerks and such like;
and many an old lady took the rickets at the
mere sound of her name. When she inflicted  a  dangerous  spell,  the  parties  had
to  send to Hamilton county for  Charley
Lee, the great witch-master to  cure  them.
This he did by shooting her picture with  a
silver ball and some other foolery.  It was a
nice sight to see this old fool set up his board
and then measure, point and cypher around
like an artillery man  planting his battery,
while the whole family were standing around
veiled and with the solemnity and anxiety of
a funeral.

None of the wizards of this county could
do anything with Eva.  They had to pale
their intellectual fires and sink into insig-
nificance before the great wizard of Hamilton County.  When a  man concluded  that
his neighbor was killing too  many  deer
around his field,  he would spell  his  gun,
which he did by going out early in the morning, and, on hearing the crack of his rifle
he walked backward to  a hickory  wythe,
which he tied in a knot in the name of the
devil.  This rendered the gun worthless until the knot was untied, or it might be taken
off by putting nine new pins in the gun and
filling it with a peculiar kind of lye, cork-

ing it up and setting it away for nine days.
One old man told me he tried this, and it
broke the spell. He had drawn right down
on a deer just before that, not over twenty
steps distant, and never cut a hair. Cows,
when bewitched, would go into mud holes
and no man could drive them out; but the
wizard, by laying the open Bible on their
backs, could bring them out; or cut the curls
out of their forehead and their tails off, and
put nine pins in their tail and burn the curls
with a poker. This would bring the witch
to the spot, and then the matter was settled
in the way our fathers settled their business. Witches were said to milk the cows
of the neighbors by means of a towel hung
up over the door, when the milk was extracted from the fringe. If such deviltry was
practiced now-a-days, the parties would be
arrested for stealing. In place of having a
herd of bob-tailed cows, we have laws
against cruelty to animals. There was an
idea, too, that if you read certain books used
by the Hard-shell Baptists, that the devil
would appear. Happily for the honor of
human nature, the belief in those foolish
and absurd pretentions has been discontinu-
ed, for forty years by an enlightened public.
Medical science has revealed remedies for
those strange diseases whose symptoms
were so little understood. The spell has

been broken from the gun forever by un-
tieing the knot of ignorance, and letting the
light of reason flood the mind. The practice
of finding water by means of a forked
switch flourished from 1850 to 1860; but
was so palpably silly that it died without
opposition.

### OF SCHOOLS.

The first schools were taught by subscription, for three months during the fall.
The first school house was built in 1825,
and others soon followed. Some of the first
school houses were built of gum logs, which
sprouted and had to be cleared about once
a year. The first teachers taught spelling,
reading and writing; but in 1840, a few fine
scholars came into the county who understood grammar and arithmetic. The free-
school law met a heavy opposition from some
of our old men, and, notwithstanding our
school system has exerted a powerful influence in civilizing the county, yet it is still
defective. We want better talent in our
teachers and more of it. A. N. Lodge, the
present superintendent, has lifted up the
sick form of our system, renovated and in-
fused new life and destiny in it, until it is in
a better condition than ever before; but it
still needs talent.

### OF SECRET ORDERS.

In 1833, Picayune Davis ran a clande-

stine Masonic lodge at his house, two miles
west of Marion. He initiated everybody,
and a gallon of whisky was the fee. All the
horse-thieves in the county belonged to this
lodge, and in that day it was a powerful
evil in shielding scoundrels and criminals.

In 1850, Fellowship Lodge of A. F. & A.
Masons was chartered in Marion. Since then
Chapter No. 100 has been chartered and a
Council also. There are now five other
lodges in the county. The Odd Fellows have
five lodges in this county. In 1856 the
Know-Nothings numbered about one hundred. In 1862 the Golden Circle reached a
membership of over eight hundred, and in
1864 the Union League numbered over twelve
hundred. In 1872, the Ku-Klux numbered
one hundred and thirty members; but the
same year they were broken up, and did not
meet again until 1874, when a few of them
formed a Klan in the west side of the county.
The Grange was introduced in 1874, and
has since spread rapidly among our farmers.

## OF LAND TITLES.

Land was the object which brought our
fathers into this wilderness, and they settled wherever they saw fit. Their first title
to the land was the "Tomahawk Right,"
which was by blazing trees around the line,
or cutting the name on a tree by a spring
on the tract. The lands lay in an irregular

shape, but all disputes were settle amicably.
After the Government survey, the Tomahawk title became worthless; but the settler had the right of pre-emption.

## OF THE PRODUCTS.

The early settlers made no change in the
county, and,consequently, there were no
products.  A people clothed in skins and de-
pending on the products of the hunt and the
spontaneous abundance of nature, could
maintain existence and a rude social organization amid the forest, without manual labor.  They lived rich in hope, but poor in
worldly goods.  Industry was consequently
paralyzed by the absence of necessity. Agri-
culture was but little encouraged for a long
time, either by the industry of the people
or the policy of the times.  It was limited to
a few patches of corn and wheat, which
were cultivated with wooden plows, and it
was as late as 1830 before the farmers produced anything for market.  Money was
very scarce.  When the few coins which the
settlers brought with them had been expend-
ed in the purchase of guns and ammunition
from Kentucky, and other places, they had
nothing to buy the necessities of life with,
say nothing of the luxuries.  So, they by mutual consent, established a custom of barter-

—F 6

ing articles of property, either at "trade
rates" or "cash price." Some articles were
very valuable and others shockingly low. A
gun from Tennessee was current at $25.00 in
trade; a sow and pigs at $2.00; a cow, at
from $4.00 to $8.00. Hamilton Corder once
bartered horses with a man and got ten
cows and calves to boot. Pretty large
boot when we consider that the cows would
now be worth more than both the horses. An
ax was sold for $4.00, and a home made one
at that.

So, anything that required a mechanic to
produce was high, but such articles as required no skillful hand to produce, were very
low. Hogs were scarce in an early day, and
it was a long time before they got a start to
raising them. They ran in the woods, and as
late as 1850 nearly everybody had what he
called his "wild hog claim." This claim en-
titled him to go into the woods and catch and
mark every hog he could, once a year. These
claims were negotiable, and were often
bought and sold; but got very cheap before
they were all extinguished. A wild-hog
claim in Big Muddy, or Pond, or Crab-Orchard bottoms was at one time very valuable;
but their conflicting claims were often the
cause of animosities, feuds and riots among
our people. Some one had marked hogs already marked, or some one had been steal-

ing and selling, and so there was a continued feud and fuss. Then it was the great hive from which sprung the innumerable number of "hog thieves" which were so common here once. But they are all gone now. The extinguishment of the claims ushered in an era of peace; feelings of safety and friendship were enkindled. For the last sixteen years this county has annually produced 1,000 hogs for market, about 1,000 head of beef cattle. During the war there were no less than 2,000 horses and mules bought in this county for Government service. It is also a sheep-producing country, and has some of the finest breeds in America. Among the mechanical productions, the first was the manufacture of hats by Aaron Youngblood, in an early day. This was followed by a shop at Bainbridge, run by Samuel Dunaway, who furnished hats for the whole country. Nearly everybody tanned their own leather. The tan-vat was a large trough, sunk to the upper rim in the ground, bark was pounded fine and put in. The hair was taken off with lime, and lard was used in place of fish oil to soften the leather, and soot to blacken it. All the shoes were home-made up to 1850; though the state of society called out every mechanical and inventive genius, yet the shoes would turn green in wet weather, and the soles try to get on top. Nearly all the wagons were made in the county, as were also the looms, wheels and farming tools.

Thousands of pounds of pennyroyal oil, mint oil, and sassafras oil are annually produced in this county. The first settlers raised a great amount of cotton for clothing. It was the main crop until 1840, when our people commenced to raise tobacco as a money crop. The usual crop of tobacco amounts to 1500 hogsheads, averaging 1500 pounds each. Cotton was extensively cultivated during the war, but now there is very little raised; the average is 400 pounds per acre. In ordinary seasons the wheat crop averages about 15 bushels per acre; corn about forty; hay about two tons per acre. Castor beans are also cultivated. And all kinds of fruits and berries have been propogated for over twenty years. Poultry is also a large source of income to our people. The sale of eggs alone reaches 40,000 dozen annually. In 1872, the Carbondale Coal and Coke Company was organized, with a capital stock of $50,000, and have been shipping coal from Carterville, in this county, at the rate of 60,000 tons per annum.

## OF PROGRESS.

The causes which led to the civilization and prosperity of this county deserve some

consideration in this book.  The state of
society and the manners of the early settlers
were indeed low enough; they were poor and
illiterate, and addicted to the rude diversions
which I have described.  So little progress
was made that, in 1826, sixteen years after
the first settlement, the total value of the
real and personal estate was only  $19,500,
or about the value of Goodall & Campbell's
storehouse.  No county in the state was settled on so little capital as was this.    The
immigrants generally paid his  last  money
for crossing the Ohio.  I have been unable to
find a man in the county worth $1,000 un-
til after 1830; but the increase  since  then
has been marvelous.  Today the county is
worth over seven millions of dollars.  The
constant travel and intercourse with other
counties gave a new current to public and
private feeling, and new life to pursuit.  The
schools and the Gospel have had  much to do
in civilizing this county; but the  enforce-
ment of good laws has been the most effective  means  of  making  men  better.
As early as 1830, the huntsmen began  to
change their clothes for those of the farmer.
Tre rude sports were giving  place to  the
more noble ambition for  mental  endowments and skill in the arts.  Industry took
the place of idleness.  The clamorous boast,
the horrid oaths, the provoking banter and

the biting sarcasm have given place to cour-
tesy and a conversation enlivened by silence
and chastened by moral culture. The three-
legged stools, moggins, trenchers and wood-
en bowls gave way to the furniture of our
day. The "tents," "lodges," wigwams,"
"stockades" and "log-cabins" have given
place to the splendid mansions that now
adorn our county. The first cabins had the
"stack" chimney, and in a few years, when
the man got able, he built another house to
the chimney, and that is why our log-houses
are double and one larger than the other.
The Benson House, in Marion, was of that
kind.

The first brick house built in the county
is in Schoharrie Prairie, and was built in
1840 by James M. Campbell. It is still
standing, but the second story was blown
down in May, 1876. It is in the most beautiful spot in the county, and ought to be
haunted, because it does not decay. The
powers of darkness must watch over it, and
by invisible means, prop its crumbling walls
and replace its falling brick. Schoharrie, so
named from the fact that a band of disguised men were once whipping a hog-thief in
it, and one of them kept crying out "Score
him, Harry!" The next brick building was
the Court House in 1841, and the Western
Exchange, in 1842. The first business house

in Marion was built by John (Bone) Davis, when the town was located. He was in such a hurry to sell whisky that he bought a set of stable logs from A. T. Benson, and put up on the square, a few feet north of the well. When the town was surveyed he fell into the square and had to move. He used to fasten his door by filling it with poles. Sterling Hill's grocery was the next, and is still standing. D. L. Pully put up a grocery on the Westbrooks corner, and J. D. Pully built "Our House,'" on the west side. John Sparks put up a hat shop on the north-east corner. The first store in the county was kept at Bainbridge in 1818, by Mr. Kipp. The next by John Davis, on the Sampson Bell place, in 1821. Then Thompson put up one where Mr. Small now lives. Coffee was 75 cents per pound, and calico 50 cents per yard. Thompson was succeeded by Warren Spiller, and he by Cripps. In 1836 Hugh Parks put up a store where Crossley now lives. In the same year, Wm. Ryburn commenced keeping goods at the Hinchcliff farm. In 1830 John Davis opened out at Sarahsville, and in 1848 John H. Mulkey and George Aiken went into business at Blairsville. In 1856 Oliver Herring had a store in Herrin's Prairie, and two years later, D. R. Harrison commenced in the same house, and is now one of the most

wealthy and respectable citizens of the
county. In 1857 Erwin and Furlong commenced business in Crab Orchard. The first
store was put up in Marion by Joshua Mulkey in 1840, the next by Robert Hooper.
Groceries were always plenty, the licenses
varying from $25.00 in 1839 to $500.00 in
1864. There have been no saloons in the
county, except at Carterville, since 1872.
General Davis, who was one of the best
friends the county ever had, ran a still-house
and saloon until in 1837, when John New-
man got drunk and the hogs ate him; and
in 1838, Essex Edmonson got drunk and
rode off into the Saline and froze to death.
About this time Davis went to the Legislature, and while there, heard A. Lincoln de-
liver a lecture on temperance. He came
home and closed the door of his saloon forever. J. T. Goddard commenced selling
whisky in Bainbridge in 1841, and finally
got to be one of the wealthiest men. Soon
after Samuel Dunaway put up a store and
is now the richest man in the county.

Marion was first incorporated in 1851,
but soon ran down. Again in 56 but again
run down. Then in 1865 by special Act, and in 1873 organized as a city
under the general laws of the State. It has
now about 1,200 inhabitants, and has eight

business houses, costing, on an average, $11,000.

Crab Orchard was incorporated in 1867, but two years afterwards disorganized. It has about 300 population.

Jeffersonville is a prosperous little village, in the north side of the county, commonly called "Shake Rag," so called from the fact that in an early day a man kept a "blind tiger" in a low, flat-roofed mud house there. When he had whisky he would stick a stick through the roof with a rag on it. As parties ascended the hill on either side, they looked to see if the rag was shaking; if not, then there was no whisky. All the whisky of that day was of the meanest kind imaginable.

Carterville is a village of 500 citizens, which sprung up on the railroad, eight miles west of Marion, and was incorporated as a village in 1873.

The first printing office in the county was owned by W. H. Wileford, in 1838. He did all the printing for this country, and in 1850 he started the *Literary Monitor*, seven miles southeast of Marion. In 1854 was started the *Marion Intelligencer*, a Democratic paper; the *Democratic Organ* in 1860-1; and the *Marion Star* in 1866. In 1866, *Our Flag*, Republican. In 1867, *Old Flag*, Democratic. In 1868, *The People's*

*Friend,* Democratic. In 1872, *Williamson County Progress,* Republican. In 1873, *Farmers' Advocate,* Independent. In 1874, *Marion Monitor,* Republican .In 1874 *Marion Democrat,* Democratic. In 1875, *Egyptian Press,* Democratic.

These papers were run for two or three years each except the *Marion Monitor* and *Egyptian Press,* which are now running, and then died for want of support. There are several good writers in the county. Among the most prominent lady writers are Mrs. M. M. Mitchell and Isabell Marschalk.

There have been four banks in this county—Agricultural Bank, Bank of Southern Illinois, in 1860, and Menahaway Bank, in 1863; Bolton Bank, in 1858.

The Agricultural Society of this county was organized May 2, 1857, with Willis Allen as President. It has since been kept up, and each year has added new proofs that the county is growing richer and better. The exhibition of the Society is second to none in Southern Illinois, except in ladies' textile work and works of art.

The Medical Association of this county was organized May 16th, 1875, by Drs. H. V. Ferrell, S. H. Bundy and A. N. Lodge, three of as learned and classic gentlemen as live in Southern Illinois. The Society now has a membership of twenty-eight, and is

highly calculated to banish quacks and igno-
ramuses from the profession, and bring talent and science to the bedside of our sick.

During the summer months, from 1850
to 1872, there were a class of men in this
county known as teamsters, who followed
the business of hauling the products of the
county to the railroads and river. In an
early day nothing could be sent to market
but such things as could walk. Ox teams
were used up to 1866, when everybody commenced to use horses for teaming. This
hauling got to be so extensive and costly that
there was a general demand for a railroad.
An Act passed the Legislature and was approved March 7th, 1867, incorporating the
Murphysboro and Shawneetown Railroad
Company, and in 1868, a petition signed by
one hundred voters, as required by said Act,
was filed with the County Clerk, asking the
Court to submit a proposition of voting
a subscription of $100,000 to the capital
stock of said company, to the legal voters of
the county. Speakers went out over the
county during the canvass, and the people
were led to believe that they were taking
stock in a railroad company, on which they
would annually draw a dividend more than
suffcient to pay the interest on the bonds
of the county. On the 3rd day of November, 1868, the proposition was voted upon,

and resulted in 1779 votes for, and 108
against subscription. On the 12th day of
December 1868, the Court made an order
that the subscription should be paid in the
bonds of the county, running for twenty
years, bearing interest at the rate of eight
per cent. per annum, payable annually at
the office of the County Treasurer. But
said bonds were not to be issued, bear date,
draw interest, or be delivered until the
road was completed and the cars running on
the same from Carbondale to Marion. Provided, if the road was not completed by the
1st day of January, 1870, this subscription
was to be void. In the same order is found
this language:

Whereas, the county of Williamson
has this day subscribed $100,000 to the
capital stock of the Murphysboro and
Shawneetown Railroad Company. Now,
therefore, for the purpose of securing
the construction and early completion
of said road, that this county make and
enter into an agreement with the M. &
S. R. R. Co., and that the said county
in and by said agreement, sell to said
Company the $100,000 stock. That the
terms of said sale and agreement shall
be in effect as follows: That when the
certificates of stock shall have been issued by said Company to said county,

the said county, after the said road
shall have been completed, and within
ten days after said Railroad Company
shall have issued to said county the
certificates of stock for said $100,000,
assign, transfer and set over to said
Company the certificates for said $100,-
000 stock so isued to said county for the
consideration of five thousand dollars,
to be paid to said county at the time of
said transfer and asignments in the
bonds of said county, issued to said
Company in payment of the subscription.

On the 12th day of December 1868,
Jesse Bishop and Addison Reece, on behalf
of the county, and Samuel Dunaway as
president of the M. & S. R. R. Company,
entered into a contract in pursuance of the
above order, to sell the stock. It was recorded at the December Special Term of
the County Court. This contract was
drawn up by Jesse Bishop. They did
not claim to have any authority from the
people for making this infamous contract,
because they gave it as their reason for
making it: "For the purpose of securing the
construction and early completion of said
road."

They did not make it in compliance with
any law or vote of the people. It has since

been urged as an excuse for the sale, that it was best for the county, that the railroad company would have closed out the stock by mortgage bonds, and the county would have got nothing. That might be a good reason to give at this day; but I have copied the motives above, which actuated the Court in its action at the time. An Act passed the Legislature and was approved March 10, 1869, to change the name of the Murphysboro and Shawneetown Railroad Company to that of the Carbondale and Shawneetown Railroad Company, and to make valid the subscription and contract of sale of the County Court. By this Act it was declared that the County Court, should, on the completion of the road to Marion, set over and transfer the certificates of stock to the railroad company without the payment of the $5,000 or any sum. This Act further provided that the interest on the bonds should be paid semi-annually in New York, in place of at the county treasurer's office. It was contended in the railroad suit described hereafter, that this Act was unconstitutional, as being *ex post facto* and impairing the obligation of contracts.

On the 24th of December, 1870, there was an order made by the Court, extending the time for the completion of the M. & S. R. R. to the 1st day of January, 1872, and also extending the time for the completion of a railroad from Carbondale to Marion, to the same time. It was contended, in the suit, that the County Court here recognized two railroad companies, and that the giving of the bonds to the latter that were voted to the former was not valid. It was also contended by the counsel in said suit that if the Act of March the 1st, 1869, was constitutional, it limited the time of the completion of said road to the 1st day of January, 1871, and it being an amended charter, could not be changed only by the Legislature. At the July special term, 1871, the Court adopted the form of a bond to be issued to the company. At this same term, July 24th, the Court, with Spain as Judge, made an order, after reciting all the Acts of the Legislature, and the previous order of this Court, and reaffirming the subscription, that the County Clerk should procure one hundred bonds of one thousand dollars each, and that on presentation of the certificates of stock by the company, the bonds should be issued and placed in the hands of James W. Samuels, as trustee, to hold until the road was completed. On this same day the Carbondale & Shawneetown Railroad Company entered into a contract with E. C. Dawes & Co. to build said road. On the 4th day of September, 1871, the Court, after

reciting the order of July the 24th, which
stated that the bonds should bear date of
January 1st, 1872, made an order that the
bonds should be prepared in blank and bear
date from the completion of the road, as
they expected to have it completed before
that date. Most people supposed that only
$50,000 worth of stock would be taken
when the road was completed to Marion,
and but few of them knew anything about
the "contract of sale;" but it had leaked out,
and by the first of November, 1871, there
was considerable talk of an injunction to
keep the Court from issuing the bonds. The
work on the road was progressing rapidly,
and Walter P. Hanchett, the agent of E. C.
Dawes & Co., became very uneasy, and on
Sunday, November 6th, 1871, sent out a special messenger to bring in the County Court.
They came in next morning, and were set
upon all that day by Hanchett and his
friends to sign the bonds and place them in
the hands of a trustee to avoid the intended
injunction from the citizens. Judge Spain
and Associate Justice Holland were opposed
to issuing the bonds until the road was completed. Manier, was for signing them.

About dark on Monday, the 7th, Hanchett and his friends got the Court together in
a room over Goodall & Campbell's store, and
tried every way to get the bonds signed.

About 12 o'clock in the night some one told
Hanchett to send for R. M. Hundley, that he
could get the Court to act.  Hundley  was
sent for, and when he came  up  town  he
went to the Lanier Hotel, where Hanchett
met him and told him what was up, and that
his assistance was urgently solicited. Hundley told him he would let him know  what
he could do in from thirty to sixty minutes.
Hundley then went over and had a talk with
the Court, and then went back, asked Hanchett what it was worth to him to  have
those bonds signed that night. He  said
one thousand dollars.  He then drew a draft
on the Carbondale Bank for $1,000,  and
left Hundley, who immediately went  home.
The Court signed the bonds that night, and
delivered them to W. N. Mitchell as trustee,
he first giving $100,000 bond for their deliv-
ery when called for.  These County Judges
were not bribed, as would seem from  this
story, because they are honest, conscientious
men; neither did  Hundley attempt to bribe
them; he simply got $1,000 to use his influ-
ence.  That they ought not to have signed
the bonds when they did is plain; but it was
an undue influence  and  not  corruption.
Mitchell deposited the bonds in a bank at
Springfield, and at the December adjourned
term, 1871, the President and Directors  of

—F 7

the railroad reported to the Court their acceptance of the road as complete from the contractors, E. C. Dawes & Co., and the Court ordered the bonds to be delivered to the company and received the certificates of stock of $100,000.

On Sunday the 14th of January, 1872, five car loads of iron were brought to Marion, and on Monday, the 15th, the last rail was laid on the track; but the cars had been running to Marion for some time before. At the special term, being the 24th day of January 1872, the Court made an order authorizing the County Clerk to assign and transfer the certificates of stock held by the county in the C. & S. R. R. Co., to E. C. Dawes & Co., of Cincinnati, Ohio, excepting $10,000 of the stock, which was to be held by the Clerk until the railroad company should have the road completed to Crab Orchard, in this county, and by the contract the railroad company was to pay $5,000 for the certificates in the bonds issued by the county in payment of the subscription, and if they had done that there would have been only $95,000 in bonds outstanding. But they paid it in money, or at least $5,000 of interest on the $100,000 of bonds. The $10,-000 of certificates are still in the possession of the County Clerk, and we pay annually $8,000 of interest and another thousand for collecting and distributing it.   At   the March term of the Circuit Court, 1873, a bill "for injunction and relief" was   filed by George Bulliner, W. M. Hindman, Henry Williams, George W. Sisney, Robert M. Allen and F. M. Maxey.   The injunction was granted by the Master-in-Chancery,   and stopped the Sheriff from collecting the railroad taxes, and the State Treasurer   from paying the interest on the bonds.   This case created a great deal of anxiety.   The case was decided by Judge Crawford against the complainants, and a judgment of $1,000 was given against them for attorney's fees. An Appeal was taken to the   Supreme   Court, and the judgment below affirmed.

In 1872, Colonel J. C. Willis, president of the St. Louis & Paducah Rail Road Company, made an earnest effort to get assistance from this county in 'building   a   road, but failed to accomplish anything.   On the 18th day of June, 1870, a vote was taken for or against subscribing $100,000 to   the capital stock of the Belleville   &   Southern Illinois Railroad Company, resulting in favor of subscription.   The Court made an   order that the subscription should be paid in the bonds of the county, running for 30 years, with 8 per cent. interest per annum. Provided, the work on the road commenced by the 1st of January, 1871, and be   completed to Marion on or before the 1st day of January, 1872; but the Court reserved the right of extending the time. And at the December adjourned term, 1871, the time was extended to the first of January, 1873; and again in December, 1872, the time was extended to the first of January, 1874. This is the last order made in the case, and of course the subscription can not now be taken. Had they built the road within the time, I doubt not but the same infamous dealings would have been played on our people, and this county would have had a debt of $200,000 wrongfully fastened upon it, instead of $100,000.

The Carbondale and Shawneetown Railroad is 17 miles long, and cost $583,407.12, and has a funded and unfunded debt of $275,890.15. For the year ending June 30th, 1875, it transported 38,959 tons of freight. The road has been honestly and fairly operated, and has been a great benefit to our county; but it is not right in principle for a majority to force an unwilling minority to contribute to the building up of a prvate person or corporation. It is right in public matters, but in private concerns their own consent ought to be obtained to make them partners or contributors.

## OF CRIMINALS.

I have now come to that division of my subject which must be more interesting to our neighbors than any other. And it is but fitting that I make a few egotistical preliminaries. I do not present this volume with the venal soul of a servile author, looking for competence or public favor. I was born a farmer, and am therefore independent. But so long as I claim the name of a citizen with my illustrious countrymen, a lasting obligation rests on me to assist in diffusing knowledge, elevating the standard of moral culture, rendering crime odious, and fastening the feelings of friendship on our people. I have intended this feeble effort to lead in that direction. I have known this people from childhood. I believe, sublimated by education, they are capable of attaining nobler hights than have usually been ascribed to the people of "Egypt." I not only glory in my birth-place, but pass encomiums on the country, and say to the world that from my knowledge of the public spirit of our people, I can expect protection, honest dealing and liberty in Williamson County. Linked to her by historic associations and proudly treasuring the memories of my fathers, the clearest duty of a modest youth like myself, whose unruly and turbulent boyhood has been subdued in the presence of this heroic people, is to assist in tearing down the curtains of darkness which hang like a mighty incubus around the crushed form of my native county, and bury them in the deep pit of contempt, where our citizens can stand by their grave forever and mutter thanksgivings to God, and invite an unsophisticated world to look with joy and pride upon a country redeemed from crime, and sparkling with brilliant gems of innocence and virtue. If I could roll back the scroll of time, and wipe from its damning record the terrible scenes of blood which have bespangled it, and restore the lives of our murdered dead, I would consider it my bounden duty, though I sailed with bloody sails on the seas of grief. But that scroll has been sealed for eternity, not to be unrolled until the echo of impartial justice shall resound in the sunlit chambers of Paradise. I make this effort, prompted by motives, to assist in redeeming, if possible, our county from under the judgment against her, and prove to the world that our community is not composed of outlaws and cutthroats, but of a highly intellectual, honorable and moral people. I could wish to write a history by which the reader would be carried along the happy gales of pleasure, and never be drifted back into the dark and bitter troubles, but I can not. Crime has darkened our county, like the shadows darken the earth, and our happiness has come to us only in fragments and detached parts. We have just passed through the deepest and crowning calamity of our history. Never was there such a shock to the feelings and sentiments of our people as the Vendetta caused. None believed that there was a heart so steeped in guilt as to conceive such crimes, nor a hand that dare commit the atrocious deeds. And yet I have to catalogue the deeds of the Vendetta, concocted by leaders and executed by fiendish emmisaries, that has not a parallel in the record of crime. Here were men at whose bloodthirstiness even savages would blush, which brands them forever as the basest and bloodiest of incarnate demons.

Tacitus said: "Shame, reproach, infamy, hatred and the execrations of the public, which are the inseparable attendants on criminal and brutal actions, are no less proper to excite a horror for vice, than the glory which perpetually attends good actions is to inspire us with a love of virtue." "And these, according to Tacitus," says Rollin, "are the two ends which every historian ought to propose to himself, by making a judicious choice of what is most extraordinary, both in good and evil, in order to occasion that public homage to be paid to virtue which is justly due it, and to create the greater abhorrence for vice on account of that eternal infamy that attends it."

Plutarch says: "But as to actions of injustice, violence and brutality, they ought not to be concealed nor disguised." Rollin himself has written, "If the virtues of those who are celebrated in history may serve us for models in the conduct of our lives, their vices and failings on the other hand are no less proper to caution and instruct us, and the strict regard which an historian is obliged to pay to truth, will not allow him to dissemble the latter through fear of eclipsing the former."

Addison has said, "The gods in bounty work up storms about us, that give mankind occasion to exert their hidden strength and throw out into practice virtues which shun the day." If these virtues are worthy of record, the conditions which generated them are certainly proper for study. This necessitates a history of the storms which the gods work up around us. By reading which, others are about to get sootiness and filth from the smoke and flames of incipient storms may take alarm and wash in the river of peace and come out white as pearls." Who that reads this record of crime will not appeal to their ruler of human fates be-

below, and record their protests in heaven
above against such slaughter!    I ask my
countrymen if crimes that have sunk a
county to the incandescent crater of perdition, ought not to be remedied.    If you
could cable the lightning from heaven, until its fiery forks kissed the flaming waves
of hell you would see nothing in its angry
flames, as they zigzag athwart the pit of
woe, throwing up a lurid glare, but the spectral mirage of murder ever standing up as a
blazing memento that "sin is death."    I am
justified by the great writers I have mentioned in giving the meanest as well as the
noblest actions of my countrymen.    If I
write of the guilty with merciless hands,
from a heart as responsive comes spontan-
eously praise for the innocent.    If not as
eloquent and touching, yet as warm, as full,
as sincere, as such a tribute deserves.    If
you are sad at the deeds of bloody men, you
will be buoyant at the faithfulness and heroism of virtuous men.    I expect out of a succession of events which possess all the traits
of tenderness, splendor, honor, crime and debauchery to write a romance without its ex-
aggerations.    It is a small difficulty to se-
lect an event, and swell it into a great tale,
by fabulous appendages and spectral productions; for he who forsakes the truth may

easily find the marvelous; but who is improved by it?

Samuel Johnson says: "Where truth is sufficient to fill the mind, fiction is worse than useless." Again, "The counterfeit debases the genuine." I am not writing a record of passions and prejudices, but of facts, with the wrapping taken off, so that they can be seen as they are. Though some of them are crimes that would make the bailiffs of hades blush and turn pale, others are heroic acts that would sweep the zones of misery away. I have abused no innocent man, nor palliated the guilt of none; but have intended that my whole course should savor of fairness and candor, more than anything else. Some have used strong arguments against our county, but I have not evaded the force of their reasoning where I was unable to refute it, either by a sweeping contempt for those who use it, or by charging them with misrepresentation, or by endeavoring to swing off the mind of the reader on some incidental point to the real condition of our county. To enter the arena of controversy with the great champions of crime, or even the little champions, is entirely beyond my ambition. Had that been my object it might have long since been effected. I do not care what this or that party may think of my feeble efforts.

I feel very little anxiety or solicitude on that subject. I have written the truth as near as I know it, and will leave the result to the arbitrament of public opinion. I have often been asked if I was not afraid that I would be killed if I wrote a history of the Vendetta. I answer, no! I have been personally acquainted with most of the supposed members of the Vendetta from childhood, and am a friend to all of them. I went to each one of them and asked him to tell me all he knew about the Vendetta, and each of them told me fully, fairly,, honestly and I believe truthfully, all I wanted to know. These people are all friendly now, and as gentlemanly as I ever met. Many of them I love and esteem, and to incur their ill-will is by no means desirable; but to court their favor at the expense of the truth or right principle would render me guilty in the sight of God, and contemptible in the estimation of all good men. Since they were so kind as to give me information enough to write the whole truth, I deem it unkind and unjust to step aside from historic facts to hurl the shafts of envy, hatred and malice at any of them. Surely they have borne enough already, and I am satisfied that if no man gets inflamed at this volume

higher than these young men, I will  still
be safe living in Williamson County.

Twenty-two of these parties are young
men like myself, and I know of no country
where finer-looking, honester, friendlier  or
more sociable young men can be found.    I
associate with them with pleasure.   Many
of them are my lasting friends, and I will
not denounce them because they have been
charged with crimes of which  they  were
not guilty.   For the guilty I have nothing
but charity; yet some of them committed
the high crime of murder without  excuse.
I shall commence with the first homicide
that occurred in the county, and give a brief
sketch of each one as it occurred, up to the
present time.   Of the smaller offenses   I
have taken no notice, though they have been
quite numerous and interesting.   Some of
them have been riots in which two or three
men have been badly wounded.   I estimate
the number of assaults to murder that have
occurred in this county at 285.    Assaults
with a deadly weapon, at 495; larceny, 190;
rape, 15; burglary, 22; perjury, 20.

The first homicide   occurred   in   1813.
Thomas Griffee was trying to shoot a bear
out of a tree where the   old   court-house
burned down in Marion, and he saw  an Indian aiming his gun at the same bear. Grif-

fee leveled his rifle at the Indian and shot him dead.

The next murder occurred in 1814. Thomas Griffee had a man working in a saltpeter cave for him, by the name of Eliott, who was a little colored. He came into Griffee's one Saturday night, and a surveyor by the name of John Hicks raised a fuss with him, and stabbed and killed him. Hicks then ran away, and at that moment a band of Indians came up to Griffee's from the camp at Bainbridge, and wanted to go in pursuit of Hicks, but Griffee would not let them go. Next morning Griffee and John Phelps started in pursuit of Hicks; they came on to him at the Odum Ford, and Hicks snapped his gun at Griffee's breast, but was taken. They took him to Kaskaskia, where the nearest Justice of the Peace lived, and he was "whipped, cropped and branded," and let go.

In 1818 a friend of Isaac Herrin came to this county and found a man dead at the Stotlar place, unwept and unknown. This man was doubtless murdered by the Indians, and if so, was the only one ever killed by them in this county.

The next murder occurred in 1821 in Rock-Creek Precinct, and was committed by Henry Parsons. It was late one evening,

when the trees were robed in the regalia of
Spring, and the great molten orb was
quenching itself in the wild winds as they
come sweeping against the rolling reach of
upland, and the gentle mist was seemingly
set to eddying by the rough elements, that
this ruffian went walking down a little
brook; his keen, restless eye kept a constant
look-out, he saw a man through the deep,
green foliage, sitting on a log across the
brook. He fired on him, and the unknown
hunter slipped off the log into the water,
never to rise again. Parsons buried him
and his gun. He used to give as an excuse
for this murder, that the Indians had murdered his father, and he intended to kill
every one of them he could find, and he
thought this man was an Indian. There never came a more infamous devil out of the
legions of horrid blackness than this man
Parsons. I give a sketch of him from the
mere love of relief. He lived unmatched in
the history of villainy; he did not seek
wealth, but lived in the woods. He was a
cold, calculating miscreant. His passions
had no touch of humanity, and his brutal ferocity was backed by a kind of brutal courage. Like an animal, he never pardoned an
affront or rivalry, and to be marked in his
tablets on either account, was a sentence of

death.  But still he was really a  coward,
and pulled the trigger of death with a hand
that shook.  His crimes were all cold-blooded, and not chargeable to passion.    Free
from rules and reckless of life, feeling no
kindness for aught that was human, hated
and dreaded by men, detested and shunned
by women, he would lay around Davis' Prairie and kill Indians.  With him the chambers of mercy had no relenting toward these
blighted men of earth, but as a wasp is ever
ready to inflict her sting, so was he ready
to commit the crime of murder.

On one occasion A. Keaster met him on
the prairie, and he threw up his gun  and
told Keaster to stop, which he did.  Soon
after he heard the keen crack of his rifle,
and then met him again.  Parsons told him
he had just killed a bear back there and he
could have it.  But Keaster knew too well
that down in the dark, thick bushes  lay an
innocent red man weltering in his own blood.
The little birds of different  species  flew
across the open space and 'back again turning and whirling in manifold gyrations over
the scene, where the ineffable glories of sun-
set had been insulted by bloody  murder.
What a scene was this! an innocent,  un-
taught man lying wounded in the bushes,
dreading the return of his slayer!    What

a thrill of joy would have electrified his soul to have seen a helping hand! Alone with his God and the winds and trees and flowers and birds, he died. The traces of his blood are hidden by the bushes and tall grass, but so long as Nature knows her own lament, will the cries of this murdered man be borne on the wild winds of heaven. I can not contemplate the character of a man 'but with astonishment that can look with fiendish complacency on the bleeding form of a brother man slain.

In 1823, Parsons killed Parson Crouch. They lived on the Crab Orchard, near the Cal. Norman bridge, and Parson bought Crouch's improvements, and was to have possession as soon as convenient; but Parsons got in a hurry, and told Crouch he must get out by Saturday night, or he would get stung with the "yeller jacket," a name for his gun. Crouch went to Equality that week for salt, and when he got within a quarter of mile of home, as he was driving along in a bit of dark and lonely forest, this sluth hound shot him dead, from behind a tree. He was found with his pockets full of toys for his little children. Parsons went to D. Odum's, threw down his gun and demanded a horse. Odum was afraid to refuse him, and he left the country.      The whole country was raised and went in pursuit, but never overtook him. He went to Tennessee, and one of his sons came to this county years afterwards and said that a black dog had always followed his father, so that he could see no peace. He died a violent death. Thus "doth Providence with secret care often vindicate herself," and justice is continually done on the trial stage of life.

In 1833, James Youngblood was at a rock quarry, on the Saline, and was making his dog kill a snake, when Gideon Alexander appeared on the bluff above and shot him through the breast. Youngblood rose and attempted to shoot Alexander, but fainted. Alexander ran down to him, helped him home, and protested that he saw nothing but a white spot down through the foliage, and thought it was a deer's tail. He waited on Youngblood constantly, and paid all bills. Youngblood lived five or six years, but finaly took to bleeding at the bullet hole, and died on the cold, damp dirt of his cabin. This was a curious case. Nothing was ever done with Alexander for this foul murder.

In 1841, Jeremiah Simmons got into a fight with J. G. Sparks, in Marion. William Benson, constable, interfered and stopped

—F 8

it. Simmons then commenced on Benson.
The latter started home, Simmons ran after him with a knife; Andrew Benson came
up at the time, ran up to Simmons   and
asked him to stop.    Simmons looked over
his shoulder and  saw who it  was,  and
stabbed backward, striking him in  the abdomen, from  which  he  died.   Simmons
made his escape.  Benson offered five hundred dollars reward and the Governor two
hundred dollars for his arrest.   In about
six months he wrote to his wife and was detected and brought back from Iowa by Benson.  He was tried and acquitted.   His
counsel were General Shields and General
McClernand.

In 1854, John Mosley killed James Burnett, by striking him on the head with  a
club.  The difficulty arose over a dog fight.
Mosley ran away and was captured in Missouri by hounds following his trail.  He was
tried and sentenced for six years, but after
one year's confinement was pardoned.

George Ramsey shot and  killed  Jack
Ward in 1859.  They had run a horse race,
and Ward had won it, which made Ramsey
mad.  He threw a rock at Ward, then when
Ward started towards him, shot him dead
and ran away, and has never come back.

In 1859, John Ferguson, then a   boy,

went out into the country and found Ellen
Reed lying in bed sick, when he shot  her
dead.  He said his father  had  too  much
business with her.  He ran away, and years
afterwards came home and soon died.

In the same year, an unknown man was
found hanging dead on the Crab  Orchard,
south of Marion.  The facts about  it  were
never  known,  but  suspicion  rested  heavily
on a man who lived near by in the bottom,
at that time.

In the spring of 1861, an Irishman passed the house of R. T. McHaney, four miles
east of Marion; McHaney came  up  about
that time and found that the man had insulted his wife.  He got his  gun  and  shot
the unknown Irishman dead.  He was tried
and acquitted on the ground  of  defending
his family.

In 1862, Reuben Stocks, a soldier in the
Seventy-Eighth Illinois Volunteers, had been
transferred to a gun-boat and  furloughed
home; he brought several of the boys with
him conducted himself rather offensively to
some people. One day he was in Blairsville,
and fell in with the "Aiken gang," some of
whom he treated roughly.  That night some
men went to his house, on the Eight Mile,
and called him up, telling  him  that  they
wanted him to go back  to  the  gun-boat.

When he went to the door, they shot him full of buckshot, from which he soon died. The perpetrators of this murder have never been discovered.

In 1862, when the One-Hundred and Twenty-Eighth Regiment left this county, and got to the Crab Orchard bridge, in Jackson county, Terry Crain got into a difficulty with John Burbridge, and struck him on the head with a stone, from which he died. Crain was not indicted until October 1875. He was arrested and admitted to bail on *habeas corpus*, in the sum of $15,000. In August 1876, he was tried, convicted and sentenced to fifteen years' confinement.

In this same year, William Stacey stabbed and killed Henderson Tippy. They were boys, bathing in the Crab Orchard, near Marion, and got to fighting. Stacey was acquitted.

In December 1862, James Baker was assassinated in Bainbridge Precinct. He walked out one night and was shot dead with a shot gun. It was thought that this was done because he was telling where deserters were.

In 1863, James Emerson, an ardent Republican, was assassinated while hunting his horses in the woods, near Blairsville. No cause for his murder is known, unless it was his politics. The assassin is unknown.

After George Aikin was frustrated in his efforts to sell out the One-Hundred and Twenty-Eighth, at Cairo, he went to Missouri, and got Allen Glide and Charley Glide, and came back here. These, and his son John Aikin, are the ones supposed to compose the "Aikin Gang." This gang flourished here in the spring of 1863, in the north part of the county, during which time several murders were committed, and no less than fifty of our citizens robbed. Dr. Bandy was taken out and whipped unmercifully, and George Cox was attacked in his house and fired on several times. This band soon got so large that it became unwieldy, and they got to stealing horses. Several of them were arrested, tried and bailed and left the country. Among the men arrested was James Cheneworth.

In 1863, six men in disguise of soldiers went to Daniel Robertson's, in Lake Creek Precinct, and told him he must go with them to hunt a deserter. He said he would if they would go by for his brother, Joseph. They did so. About one and one-half miles from Joseph's, one man fired on Daniel, the ball striking him in the forehead, and he fell dead. Then, all six fired on Joseph, shooting four holes in his clothing, but he jumped from his horse and made his escape. They turned back, went to Peter Wascher's, and fired at him, and he at them, and he escaped. It was supposed to be some of his gang.

In 1863, James Stilly was killed by Ben Batts. The latter was working in his field, and Stilly came to him and they got into a fight, when Batts killed him with a hoe, and ran away.

In the same year, William Moulton was killed by some unknown assassin. Joshua McGinnnis, Dock Dickson, Thomas Murray and Henry Norris were arrested for this offense, but there being no evidence, they were acquitted. McGinnis may have been guilty, but the others were not.

One morning in 1864, Samuel Moore was found dead at the door of a saloon in Jeffersonville. Parties had been drinking late the night before, and some one had killed him with a club. A man by the name of Washum was indicted, tried and acquitted; and his blood is unexpatiated to this day.

During this year, Vincent Hinchcliff shot and killed James Pickett, a young lawyer of Grassy Precinct, at Blairsville. Pickett was appearing in a case against the administrator of William Hinchcliff's estate, and he and Vincent got into a fight, with the result

I have mentioned. Vincent was tried and acquitted on the ground of self-defense.

The last homicide of this year occurred on the 24th day of March. Several of the Parkers and Jordans got into a general fight in Marion, over an old feud, and William C. Parker shot and killed Richard Jordan. Two or three others were wounded. Parker ran away and has never been caught.

In 1865, Isham Canady was shot and killed, in Marion, under circumstances of such a justifiable nature, as to render the homicide almost an improper incident for a catalogue like this, because the killing was not the result of malice, but of a combination of circumstances which made it absolutely necessary at the very moment. The defendant was tried and acquitted on the ground of self-defense.

The next homicide of the year was that of Christopher Howard, who was assassinated near Herrin's Prairie, on Sunday, by some unknown villain, supposed to be on account of politics. He was a Republican.

In 1866, William L. Burton and Samuel McMahan were both shot and killed in a general fight in Sulphur Springs. The fight grew out of politics. They were both Republicans. Dixon B. Ward was indicted for the killing, but there was no evidence of his guilt and he was acquitted.

In 1867, Horace Sims and John Latta got into a rough-and-tumble fight, at Sim's Mill, on the Saline, and Sims stabbed Latta in the thigh, from which he bled to death. Sims was tried and acquitted on the grounds of self-defense, he being on the 'bottom at the time.

During this year, John Cheneworth was assassinated in the woods, near his house, in Herrin's Prairie. He was not found until several days after. Mr. Cheneworth was a still, quiet gentleman. William Chitty and one of his sons were arrested for the crime, but there was not a shadow of evidence against them.

At the November election, 1868, a shooting scrape occurred between the Stanleys and Cashes, in Southern Precinct, in which several shots were fired, and Wm. Stanley was killed. Isiah Cash was accused of the crime, but the evidence tended to show that another man was guilty. This was an old family feud, warmed up by politics, the Stanleys being Republicans. In 1870 Isiah Cash was driving along on his wagon, when he was assassinated, fourteen buckshot piercing his body. His slayer has never been known, but enough is known to say that suspicion has rested on the wrong man.

One summer night in 1868, Charles

McHaney and a 'boy by the name of Rogers got into a fight, five miles east of Marion, when Rogers stabbed and killed McHaney. He was tried and acquitted on the ground of self-defense.

In 1869 George Mandrel, a lunatic in Northern Precinct, met his father in the road and slew him with an ax. The scene was a bloody one, and Mandrel's lunacy is the only thing that saved his neck.

On the first day of January, 1869, Samuel Cover shot and killed Phillip Thompson Corder in Marion. The difficulty arose about a difficulty between Cover and a brother of Corder's. Corder was striking at Cover with brass nuckles, when he was shot. Cover was then put in jail to keep him from being mobbed. He was afterwards tried and acquitted on the ground of self-defense.

On the first day of December, 1868, William Barham shot and killed Andrew J. Lowe, in Marion. Barham was a young man, afflicted with lunacy, and while in this condition stepped into Mr. Lowe's saloon, and shot him in the forehead. Barham was arrested by B. F. Lowe, and lodged in jail. On the 7th day of September, 1869, he broke jail and escaped. Five years afterwards he was betrayed by a young lady in Tennessee, and arrested by Thomas Ballou, and brought to Marion. He was tried, found guilty of manslaughter, and sentenced for one year.

In 1870, Thomas Pinkey White, a prominent citizen of Herrin Prairie, was seen crossing his field in his shirt sleeves. He was never seen again. At the back of the field where he went out, were signs of violence—a little blood and the tracks of two horses from there to Muddy River. It is evident that he was assassinated, but there are some who do not share this opinion. No cause for his running away was known to exist to anybody. He was an outspoken Republican, and his conduct in this line made him some enemies.

In 1871, Mastin G. Walker, an old and respected citizen of this county, living seven miles northeast of Marion, was met on his farm by a ruffian, beaten over the head with a barrel of a gun, and slain. John Owen, an old man (one of his neighbors, with whom he had some trouble about land), was arrested, tried, convicted and sentenced for twenty-five years to prison; and is now at Joliet.

In 1871, Valentine Springhardt got into a difficulty at a mill in Marion, and was struck on the head with a large wrench and killed. The defendant gave himself up and was afterwards tried and acquitted on the ground of self-defense.

On the 15th day of April 1872,   Isaac Vancil, the first white man born in this county, a man seventy-three years old, living on Big Muddy, was notified to leave the county or suffer death.  He did not obey the order, and on the night of the 22nd, ten men in disguise of Ku-Klux, rode up to the house, took him out about a mile down the river bottom, and put a skinned pole in the forks of two saplings and hung him, and left him hanging.  Next morning he was found, and all around was still, blank and lifeless.   I suppose that it must be a source of but little satisfaction to that infamous herd of desperate men to look upon that horrible scene, and feel and know they are the guilty authors.  They are hid from the face of men, but a just, certain, inexorable retribution awaits them.  In the last day, God will make requisition for the blood of Vancil, which has stained Heaven with its vulgar blot.  Until then we must submit to the arbitrament of time, and calmly wait with patience and resignation the unbiased inquest of the future.

I know nothing of Ku-Klux, but conclude that they are bound by abhorrent oaths, for a squadron of devils could not drive them from their allegiance.  It is a hard thing for

a man to swear blind allegiance and implicit
servitude to a master over both soul and conscience, and never again feel the pure, un-
tainted, dashing blood of freedom course his
natural veins.  Who can succumb to such a
disgraceful yoke?  Leon in his holy indig-
nation could make no greater demand than
this.  A den of these infernal demons holding their hellish, midnight rivelry, with their
blood-shot eyes glaring with untold crimes,
and their haggard visages bloated with  an
impress that tells of woe and mean distress,
must be a nice gathering! It may be that
some old bridge, on some lone creek,  could
tell a tale of a soul in mortal strait, and the
constellation of the weeping Hades dropped
tears on a scene like this, where the trees
have plead for mercy for some other man in
the clutches of these men, sneaking,  low-
down, white-livered  scoundrels.    Vancil
was an honest, hard-working man, but had
some serious faults.  Still,  God  gave  an
equal right to live and none the  right to
deal death and ruin in a land of peace. Soon
after his death eighteen men were arrested
in Franklin county, charged with the murder; 'but were acquitted.  Pleasant G. Veach,
Francis M. Gray and Samuel Gossett  were
then arrested in this county, and admitted to
bail in Benton.  In a few days, Jesse Cavens,

Wm. Sansom, Samuel Sweet, Jonas G. Ellett
and John Rich, of this county, were arrested and lodged in jail at Marion. In eighteen days, Ellett and Gossett were bailed,
and the others sent to Perry County jail,
where they remained until December, when
they were all tried in Franklin county, on
change of venue, and acquitted. Some of
these parties were indicted in the United
States Court at Springfield, under the Ku-
Klux Act, but all came clear. Colonel Am-
brose Spencer prosecuted them, and he was,
on the 6th of January 1873, arrested for
having them falsely imprisoned, and put in
jail himself for a short time, and Jonas G.
Ellett got $4,000 damages against him in
this county.

In 1872, James Myers was hauling, near
his house on the Eight Mile, when he was
shot from behind a tree with a shot-gun. He
was taken to his house, and Samuel Tyner,
one of his step-sons, with whom he had had
a few words, was there and asked him what
he could do for him. Myers told him to go
for a doctor. He went to Dr. Hinchliff,
and told him where Myers was shot, when
he had no time to find out. He had the day
before borrowed a gun from Dr. Hinchliff,
and it was found the next day where he had
hid it. Young Tyner was arrested and admitted to bail. Myers not being dead, he

ran away and has never been found. Myers died soon after.

In August 1872, Richard Allison shot and killed Samuel Absher, in a fight which arose about some chicken-coops, in Rock Creek Precinct. Allison ran away, and has never been caught. He stands indicted for manslaughter.

In April 1873, Francis M. Wise and William Newton, of Saline, were riding along the highway together. They had bartered mules, and Wise wanted to rue, but Newton would not. Wise then shot him dead from his horse and made his escape. He is indicted for the crime of murder.

In 1874, James Gibbs and Dock Burnett, two young men, got into a fight at a party, seven miles south of Marion. They agreed to fight fair, and walked out with seconds. Bennett had a knife handed to him, with which he stabbed and killed Gibbs. Young Gibbs stood up and fought desperately with his fist, while Burnett was cutting him to pieces. He fell, and a cry went up to Heaven from the more tender-hearted in the crowd, at the cruel murderous exhibition. Burnett fled the county, and a reward of $500 was offered for his arrest.

September 17, 1874, Stewart Culp, a respectable citizen of this county, was on his way from DeSoto, when he was shot and killed. He lay in his wagon with his head and one arm hanging out. His neck seemed to be broken. His horses went home with him in that condition. Nothing is known of his murderers.

During this same year, William Meece was assassinated by Samuel Keeling, who shot him in the back at church in Northern Precinct. They were both young men, and had had a fight a few days before. Keeling escaped, and one year afterwards he was arrested in Kansas by John Fletcher, and brought back to Marion. He changed the venue in his case to Saline county, and was tried and sentenced for life to prison.

The next homicide that occurred in this county was that of Capt. James B. Murray, who was walking along a street in Marion, when he came to where Leander Ferrell was sitting. He made a halt, and was fired on by Ferrell. Several shots were exchanged between them, and Murray fell, mortally wounded, and died next morning. Ferrell was arrested and bailed on *habeas corpus*, and was tried in 1876, and acquitted of manslaughter. Murray was a large, powerful man, cool and deliberate, but a man of the greatest courage. Ferrell has been a quiet, peaceable citizen. They had several difficulties before, in which Murray came near killing Ferrell.

In the summer of 1876, John Kelly and Samuel Lipsy got into a fight in Carterville, and Kelly stabbed Lipsy in the back. Lipsy afterwards died, and it is now claimed from the effects of the wound. Kelly is in jail awaiting a trial.

I have now come to those troubles which were known as

## "THE BLOODY VENDETTA,"

And first, I will give an account of the families that have been suspected of belonging to the Vendetta. And first of the Russells: Philip T. Russell, who settled on the Eight Mile Prairie in 1817, brought with him three sons, James, Samuel and Jefferson. Jefferson Russell's family consisted of himself and wife, and eight children: Harriet, Winifred, Scott, Nancy, Adelade, Mary, John R., Thomas J., and Hope. Four of these girls are married, but none of this family have been implicated in the Vendetta but Thomas .They are among our wealthiest and most respectable farmers, possessing good intelligence and education, and none of them ever did anything to bring reproach upon themselves, except it was Thomas. They live in the center of the Eight Mile, on the west side of the county, in a large

residence, surrounded by the conveniences
of life.

The Sisney family consisted of George
W., who first married Panina Brown, and
had four children who are now living: Winfield S., John, George W., Jr., and Martha
Jane. The latter is now eighteen years old.
Mrs. Sisney died in 1863, and Sisney then
married Miss Fredonia Williams, who now
has four small children. Winfield married
Miss Malissa Williams; John Miss Molie
Higgins; George, Jr., Miss Hannah Tippy.
Sisney was a man of more than ordinary
ability; was medium size and compactly
built, dark complexion, a very passionate
and fearless man, but high-toned, generous
and open-hearted. He served as captain in
the Eight-First Illinois Volunteers, and was
one of the number who volunteered to run
the blockade at Vicksburg. In 1866 he was
elected Sheriff, and again ran in 1874, but
was defeated. At his death he had accumulated property to the amount of several
thousand dollars. In 1872 he wrote some
sensible articles against the stock law, and
argued that it would benefit him, but would
be a hardship on the poor farmers. The
young Sisneys received common school educations and stand well in this county for
honesty and fair dealing.

—F 9

Of the Hendersons, Joseph Henderson of Kentucky, had three sons who came to this county: William, Joseph W., and James. William has seven children: Felix, James, Pad, John, Emma, Margaret and Nancy. Margaret and Nancy are married. Joseph W. has six children: Samuel, William, Thomas, Synoma, Lucy and Dike. James had but one child, Granite, eleven years old. Joseph W. came to this county in March, 1864, and William, March of 1865. Samuel and James, Jr., served four years in the Twentieth Kentucky Union Volunteers. James, Sr., the leader, was born on the head-waters of Blood River, Kentucky, and was forty-four years old when he was killed. He was raised on a farm, but never worked one until he came to this state. When a boy, he drove a team, and one day got drunk, and from that day until his death he never drank a drop of liquor. He then went to Missouri, and then to Texas, and back to Kentucky, and lived with his brother William. In 1851 he went to California, and remained seven years, and came back to Kentucky with $6,000, and followed buying and selling notes until 1860, when he went to peddling tobacco; his brother John manufacturing it. Felix G. traveled with him all over the Southern States. In Guntown they saw seven men hung for opinion's sake. James' in-

dignation was excited, and he declared he
would go home and join the Union army.
He left his bills uncollected, and went to Paducah and got permission to raise a company.  This company he raised by going
around in the bushes at night.   The gun-
boats met him, by agreement, up the river,
and took his company to Paducah, and he
joined the Twentieth Kentucky Infantry.
He then went up the river and captured the
Agnew ferry-boat, which he piloted down
the river himself.  But, not being a pilot, it
sometimes took the brush on  him.   After
four months' service, he procured a substi-
tute and started out with five men as a spy.
On this raid he captured eleven rebels, and
among them, Captain Bolen, who now  lives
in Paris, Henry County, Tennessee.   He
next acted as guide, and conducted General
Smith's brigade to Fort Henry.  After this
he left the army, and  moved into  Massac
county, Illinois.  Here he  remained  one
year, and then joined the Fifth Iowa Cavalry as guide, in which capacity he served
for eight months, and was then guide  for
General Lowe.  He was in a  skirmish  at
Clarksville, and in chasing one man whom he
knew, shot at him, and cut a lock of  hair
from his head, which he picked up and kept.
The man came to Marion with Hendricks,
from Kentucky, when he had a suit against

Henderson, and they had a hearty laugh over it. While he was with the Fifth Iowa he took a few men and went out from Fort Henry where a man was harboring five rebels. When Henderson got there they were all in the lot but Captain Ozburn, of Callaway County, Kentucky, who was standing at the gate. Henderson told him to surrender, Ozburn said nothing, but drew his revolver, when Henderson shot him, and walked up to him, and Ozburn fell into his arms. Henderson not thinking he was hurt, again called on him to surrender. Poor Ozburn surrendered his life to his Maker, and sank, and died at his feet. He came to this county February 1864, and in October 'bought the land, then in the woods, on which he died. Henderson was a large man, weighing over two hundred pounds, and without doubt the most powerful man, physically, in this county. He could not read, but was a coherent thinker; shrewd, cunning, and cautious; a man of but few words, but pleasant and child-like in manners, making him a very safe friend, but a dangerous enemy. Such is the man who was the reputed leader of the Russell side of the Vendetta. Felix always lived with James until within two or three years before his death. Some of the Henderson girls are very handsome, and are excellent school teachers. The men are mostly illiterate, but shrewd and cunning. They have dark skins, coal black eyes and raven hair, and some of them are fine-looking men. They are men of few words, and are not the kind of people that turn over mountains, but a braver set of men don't live on earth. With the exception of Pad, they are considered honest and fair in all their dealings.

This comprises the leading families on the Republican side of the Vendetta. Many others are implicated in the bloody feud with them but I will describe them as they come upon the scene.

The Bulliner family consisted of George Bulliner, his wife and eleven children. Elizabeth, Mary, Nancy Emeline, Rebecca Adeline, David, John, Monroe, George, Emannal, Amanda Jane and Martha Lane. The youngest is now sixteen years old. Elizabeth married Jordan C. Halstead; Mary, John Gamble; Nancy, W. N. Berkley; Rebecca, Aaron Smith; Amanda, Pierce Crain; Monroe married Miss Josephine Council, a very handsome and accomplished lady; Emanuel married Miss Mary Tiner, and David, at his death was engaged to Miss Cornelia O'Neal, of Tennessee. George Bullner lived in McNair county, Tennessee, and was a man of considerable means and influence. At the breaking out of the war, he was a loyal man, and in September 1862, raised what was always after known as "Bulliner's Company," They first served as state guards, and finally entered the Union Army. Bulliner served without pay. He came to this county on the 28th day of January, 1865, and bought a farm from Arthur Blake, two miles southeast of the Egiht Mile, on which stood a two-story brick residence. In 1876 he put up a horse-mill and a cotton-gin. His son, David, first kept store with F. M. Sparks, a half-mile north of his house, and then put up a store at home. This he kept a few years, and then moved to Crainville, and went in with Wm. Spencer, to whom he afterwards sold out, and with whom he had a little suit, but not one that generated ill-feelings. The other boys worked on the farm, and are young men of fine personal appearance, light complexion, dark hair, social, jovial and very pleasant in their manners and address. George Bulliner was a man of more than ordinary ability, a large, stout-built man, of homely appearance. He was noted for his zeal for what he regarded as right, for his sterling honesty and boldness in asserting and maintaining his opinion, and defending his principles. He was energetic, and a shrewd business man, and was kind and lenient to the poor, buying what ever they had to sell; and in building up the country, and helping his neighbors, he not only became wealthy, but built up a character that was conspicuous and honorable. To a stranger he appeared like a cross, ill-natured man; but that was not his nature. He was not a religious man, and sometimes resorted to rough sports and amusements. At the time of his death he was sixty-one years old.

The Hinchcliff family consisted of William Hinchcliff, who settled here in an early day and died in 1858, his wife and three sons: Vincent, Robert and William. As a family, they are very intellectual, and noted throughout this county for integrity and his social qualities. They live on a farm on the north side of the Eight Mile, a half-mile from Russell's. They used to keep store there, and Vince was a physician, a good musician and a man of fine ability, but of a very violent temper. He was agreeable and social to his friends, but unpleasant and offensive to his enemies, growing out of politics. Robert is a man very different in temper. Educated, refined, a splendid musician, sociable, honest, and a gentleman from the ground up. He is also an artist, and paints with great skill. He lives in a lovely little cottage amid bowers where roses, honeysuckle and jessamines mingle their colors and rich perfumes with the poseys and daisies. A meadow in its green livery, with tall, wild flowers oscillating in the breeze, and fields and forests so bended as to make a landscape of every varying beauty, surrounds his house, where the song of the little bird is pouring forth, and insects sport playfully in mid-air, which makes their bright hues appear more resplendent by the sun's golden rays. Near the cottage is a flower-garden, containing every thing that can charm the eye or delight the senses. I will not attempt to describe the little floral world, for there is no end to it. This is a picture of his home, and imagination can furnish nothing more delightful than a life gliding away amid a scene like this. Robert and William have never had anything to do or say in the Vendetta, but both have been studiously exonerated from all suspicion by all parties.

The Crain family is a very large one. Spencer and Jasper Crain settled in this county in an early day. Spencer had several children; among them was Jasper, U.; Jasper, Sr., had several, among them was William and Spencer, Jr. William Crain had eight children: Nancy Ann, George F., Terry, alias "Big Terry," Noah W., alias "Yaller Bill," William J., alias "Big Jep," Warren, Marshal T., Wesley. Jasper U. Crain has seven children: Terry, Samuel R., Lorenzo, Alonzo, Mary, Pierce, Eva.

Spencer Crain, Jr., had three living children, Wm. J., alias "Black Bill," Martha, and Elizabeth.

The other families are too numerous to name. Then, in fact, it would be useless, as only five of those I have mentioned have been implicated in the Vendetta. Most of the Crains are religious, and live honest, pay their debts, and deal fairly with their neighbors. William and some of his boys would often get into rough-and-tumble fights; but never used weapons. "Big Terry," now dead, was a powerful man. Aside from this, there was nothing to distinguish them from the rest of our citizens. George F. is a Justice of the Peace, and one of the most respectable and honorable citizens of the county. The same could be said of several others of them. They received common school educations, and none of them are very wealthy; but all are good livers, and farmers, and live three miles east of the Eight Mile. They belong to the sanguine temperament (excepting Black Bill who is bilious) and are social and agreeable men to meet. These are the leading families on the Democratic side. I will give account of others as they appear on the scene. The first difficulty in the Vendetta occurred on Saturday, the 4th of July 1868, in a saloon one and a half miles east of Carbondale; but it is right to say that there is not a drunkard, excepting Samuel Music, in all the Vendetta. Felix G. Henderson was on his way from Carbondale, about 4 o'clock p. m. It was raining very hard, and he stopped in the saloon, where the Bulliners, for the same reason, had stopped a few minutes before. The Bulliners were playing cards. After a while George Bulliner bantered "Field" for a game. They went to playing. Presently George Bulliner, Jr., (a son of David Bulliner) of Tennessee, commenced by betting on the game, and got to putting in. Field told him to shut up, that it was none of his business. Young George said Bulliner was six and "Field" five. "Field" said he was six and Bulliner five. Bulliner said "Field" was right. "Field" then got up and called young George a dam lying son of a——— Young George first got a chair, which was taken from him, and then they clinched. George broke away and got some bottles "Field" drew his knife, and George Bulliner, Sr., struck him with a bottle, and knocked him six or seven feet. A general fight followed, in which "Field" was badly beaten up. The bar-keeper's wife and James Russell parted them. At this time, "Field" did not know the Bulliners, and asked who they were. In the fight, "Field" had cut David Stancil on the arm. Next day Stancil sent

Eli Farmer to Henderson to apologize for him. When Farmer came James Henderson cursed "Field," and told him that a saloon was no place to be in. After the fight was over, "Field" fearing the Bulliners would follow him, went an unusual route to William Hindman's in this county, where George Sisney washed off the blood. "Field" did not feel satisfied, so next week he went to where young George was plowing in David Stancil's field. They spoke, and Bulliner asked him how he was getting, and if he was hurt. "Field" said:

"I am bodily hurt. I was overpowered the other day, and if you want to try it over I am willing, any way you want to." Bulliner said that he did not want to fight. "Field" told him that he had an equal show now, and that he himself had been mobbed. Bulliner, fearing that Henderson was going to shoot him, broke for a tree and called for his pistol. Henderson told him that he came to offer him a fair fight, and rode off home. In the September following, Bulliner had three ricks of hay burned. The tracks of two persons were observed leading in the direction of Carterville. The next week his cotton-gin was burned and had at the time one hundred thousand pounds of cotton in it, fifteen thousand pounds of which were taken out of ruins, a week after the fire.

Suspicion was thrown by some on Felix, but a large majority at that time supposed it was incendiaries from Tennessee, and it is not known to this day who did commit this arson.

In 1872 Thomas J. Russell and John Bulliner commenced going alternately with Miss Sarah Stocks. They soon became cool rivals. Bulliner finally succeeded in making himself the most acceptable visitor. Envy seized Russell, and they became enemies; but other than a few short words, had no difficulty until the riot at Crainville.

In 1869, a man by the name of Samuel Brethers, who lived at Bulliner's, cultivated a part of Sisney's farm, which joined Bulliner on the east. He raised a crop of oats, and after they were thrashed, he left them on Sisney's farm. He then sold the oats to Sisney to pay the rent, and also sold them to David Bulliner, to pay a debt, and went to Texas. Bulliner claimed the oats, and replevied them from Sisney, but got beat in the suit. On the 26th day of April, 1870, they met at Sisney's blacksmith shop to settle. They differed about each other's account, and Sisney said, "If we can not agree we will leave it to our 'betters." David said, "I tried you in law once." Sisney replied "Yes! and I beat you." David said "Yes! and you did it by hard swearing;"

and Sisney knocked him down with a shovel.
David ran home, got his father, John and
Monroe with their pistols, and started
back. Sisney, on seeing them coming, retreated out the back way, from his house,
with a Henry rifle. John fired on him,
near the house, at about 15 yards. David
fired with a gun, and again at 250 yards,
just as Sisney went behind an old tree that
stood in the field. Four of the balls took effect in his leg and hip. Sisney then asked
for quarters, and George Bulliner stopped
his boys, Sisney was carried to his house,
and Bulliner waited on him faithfully for
several days. They were all indicted in September following, and four of the Bulliners
and Sisney each fined $100. This was the
only difficulty that occured between the
Sisneys and the Bulliners.

I have now given the three orginal causes of the Vendetta; first a deck of cards;
second a woman; third, oats. The Crains
next came into the scene in a fight against
the Sisneys. Marshal T. Crain and John
Sisney had had a fight eight years before,
but had made it up. Still later, they had
another fight, at Mrs. Clements, about some
"tales." John was accused of striking
Marshal with brass knuckles. They, at
this time, agreed never to be friends again,
yet not to fight any more; but in Novem-

ber, 1872, they got at it again, with "Big Jep" and Wash, (George, Jr.,) Sisney, thrown in for strikers; but nobody was hurt.

About the 15th day of December, 1872, James Henderson went into the Company store, in Carterville, and bought a pair of boots, and a dog fight occured at the door, in which the Crain boys had a dog. "Big Terry" was cursing Elijah Peterson for interfering. Henderson thought that they took the other dog to be his, but he said nothing, and started off. "Big Terry" said:

"I would like to knock that dam black rascal."

Henderson, not thinking the remark intended for him, walked on, when Terry added,

"That rascal with the boots."

James told him it was a good time, to "lam in." A few more words were passed, but no fighting. This affair threw the Hendersons and Crains into line against each other. The Crains, now being enemies of the Sisneys and Hendersons, become pliant allies to the Bulliners.

On the 25th day of the same month the Carterville riot occurred. John Sisney, Wesley and Marshal Crain were in the Company Store, when Sisney threw out some banter to Marsh, who struck him three times with a weight. Milton Black started towards them, and "Big Terry" told him not to interfere, that they were boys. Black said he would not. Then Terry said:

"I am a better man than you, Black."

Black said, "That is untrue."

Terry said, "I am going to whip you."

Black replied, "You ain't done it."

Terry started at him, and Black knocked him down three times, and it was supposed with brass knuckles. The other Crain boys started towards Black, and George Sisney cried out:

"Give Black fair play."

Just then some one knocked him (Sisney) senseless to the floor, and Warren Crain fell on him. They fought around for a while, and then got outside; the fight stopped, and, after a few words, Wesley Council struck Sisney on the forehead with something in his hand, supposed to be a weight. After that the Sisneys and Blacks went into Black's grocery, when Terry again came on to Black, but George Bulliner interfered, and said Black should not be imposed upon, and there it had to stop. Sisney and Black went to the hotel to wash, when Terry and posse came in to arrest Black for using knuckles. Black resisted, saying that a private citizen had no right to arrest him. This ended the riot. Some of the parties were arrested, and their trial

set for December 30th, at Crainville.   The
Hendersons had heard that the Crains had
said, if any of them came down on that day
they would be to haul home.  So, on that day
all the Hendersons, Sisneys, Bulliners,
Crains, Council, Thomas Russell, some of
the Stotlars, and several others, were on
hand, and, in place of a trial by law, they
had a trial by wager of battle.  Russell raised a difficulty with John Bulliner.  They
commenced fighting on the east side of Wm.
Spence's store, and fought around to  the
south door, John with a little stick,   and
Tom with his fist.  James Henderson  told
Tom to get a brick, which he did and threw
it at Bulliner, who then drew his pistol. Russell then drew his.  At this instant David
Bulliner came out of the store, and  James
Henderson drew a revolver about  a  foot
long, and said no man should touch him. The
Bulliners then went into the house,  where
some of the Crain boys were.   Sam Henderson struck the house with his fist, and
asked:

"Where are those God d———n fighting
Crains that were going to whip the  Hendersons?"

James H. said:

"I can whip any man on the ground."

George Bulliner, standing in  the  door,
said:

"Henderson, I don't know so much about that, that is hard to take."

Henderson told him to come out and fight like a man.  Bulliner said he had nothing against the Hendersons.  James said:

"I have against you; you beat my nephew."

"Field" spoke up and said:

"I am the one; come out and fight a man of your size."

Bulliner started out, but was caught by Wm. Spence, who shoved him back and shut the door.  Henderson cursed around for half an hour, calling the Crains traitors, cowards, &c., and then went home, alleging that the Bulliners and Crains were so thick in Spence's cellar, that when they drew their breath the floor raised.  Marshal Crain was indicted for an assault with a deadly weapon on John Sisney, but never had a trial.  The State's Attorney filed an information against about twenty of these fellows for riot, and at the February term of the County Court, 1873, they were all in Marion.  The information was quashed.  Thomas Russell went back to Crainville, and at Spence's store he met with three of the Bulliner boys.  They soon determined on a fight, but Russell ran off to Carterville, a half mile, where he found the Hendersons.

—F 10

He told James to go back with him and see
him a fair fight. James started back in a
wagon, and they met George Bulliner coming down. James got out of his wagon and
said:

"Bulliner, you are the cause of all this
trouble; why don't you make your boys 'be-
have, and let people alone?"

Bulliner said he could not control them.
James said:

"That's a lie; get down and let us stop
it, for you are heading it; let's fight it  out
'between me and you, and stop it, or, stop it
without fighting, just as you want to."

Bulliner said he was for peace. So they
agreed to have no more fighting.

Soon after this Henderson was driving
along by Vincent Hinchcliff's with a load
of rock, when Bulliner overtook him and
they had some very  hot  words,  Bulliner
threatened to kill him on the spot, and Henderson challenged him to  fight.   Behind
Bulliner was a wagon with five others in it,
but they said nothing.  Henderson drove on.
He always contended from that day that he
was waylaid.  And it is almost certain  that
Bulliner had been before this.

Along in the summer of 1873, Marshal
Crain and John Sisney met  in  Carterville
one night, and talked about shooting   each

other, but put their pistols away without firing.

Jennings, the State's Attorney, had these rioters arrested four times, and the information for riot was as often quashed. On the fifth trial, some of the rioters on the Crain side were convicted; those on the other side changed venue to Jackson county, where they were acquitted. At one of these attempted trials George Sisney got mad at Jennings, and was cursing him to me, in the County Clerk's office, when Wesley Council stepped in at the door. Sisney called him a "hell cat." Council drew his revolver, and I caught him and told him he should not be hurt. Sisney drew his revolver, but could not shoot without striking me, which he would not do. Wash Sisney was present, and did some talking of a threatening character. Council behaved himself with remarkable coolness to be in the presence of a man of the nerve of Sisney. I got him out of the door, and he went into an adjoining house. After the danger was all over, there were some wonderful exhibitions of bravery among the outsiders. The next difficulty in the Vendetta was Nov. 6, 1873, at the election in the Eight Mile, when Thomas Russell, David Pleasant and David Bulliner got into a fuss over an old feud, and James Norris, a new actor on the stage, (as was also

Pleasant) who worked for the Bulliners, took it up for Bulliner. He went for B's for a gun and soon returned with one, and Tom drew his revolver, but parties interfered, and prevented any killing. This was a serious affair. It was two desperate young men on each side, facing each other with deadly weapons, and it took the greatest exertion to prevent the death of some of them.

On the morning of December 12, 1873, George Bulliner started to Carbondale, on horseback. The sun was standing against the murkey haze of the east, red and sullen, like a great drop of blood. The pearly, vapor-like sails dotted the sky, and covered the more delicate sculptured clouds with their alabaster sides. The great oak trees lifted their parapets to the morning sky, and spangled the earth with shadows. The voiceless winds swept with sublime resignation lawless through the leafless woods, and a melancholy breeze stirred the dead ferns and droping rushes. A cold-scented sleuthhound had followed the tracks of Bulliner remorselessly. This morning two of them, with stealthy movement, took their position near the Jackson county line in an old tree top, on the ground. There, planted on the spot, their ears drank in every sound that broke the air, mouth half open, ears, eyes, soul, all directed up the road to catch, if

possible, each passing object. They thought
they could tell the thud of Bulliner's horse's
feet from all others. They lay down on their
breasts, and fixed their eyes on the  road
winding down the valley.   They stuck up
brush to shield them from observation, like
an Indian watching for his  victim,  alertly
awake to every noise.  Bulliner came riding
along and one of the assassins fired on him;
only two or three of the balls took effect in
his hip and leg; but his horse wheeled and
threw his back to the assassins, who fired
on him again, and forty-four buck-shot took
effect in his back, and he fell to the earth.
The assassins then escaped.  Bulliner was
soon found and carried to the nearest house,
and his sons notified, but after desperate
riding John reached the place only in time
to hear his father say, "Turn me over and
let me die." He did so, and George Bulliner escaped from the cruelties of earth to
the charities of heaven.  Look here, all you
infernal wretches, and contemplate a spec-
tacle which should inflame our hearts with
mercy.   Right in the face of heaven,  and
among men, George Bulliner was slain 'by
one of the most sordid mortals that  ever
disgraced the black catalogue of crime,  or
befouled  the name of civilization, and his
death, today, is unexpiated in  Williamson
County.

On the night of the 27th of March 1874, while Monroe and David Bulliner were on their way home from church, about half a mile westward from their home, in a lane, they were fired on by two assassins, who were concealed in the fence corners, about twenty feet apart. The balls went in front of their breasts. David stepped forward a few steps, both drew their revolvers and commenced firing on the assassins. A perfect hurricane of shots followed. The people going home from church knew what it meant, and they stood still. The assassins emptied two double-barrel shot guns and two navy revolvers. David fired three shots, and Monroe six. The last shot from the assasin's gun struck David in the back, and he cried out, "I'm shot!" and at the same time heard a voice further down the road. He asked who was there; a voice replied, "The Stancils." Mrs. Stancil, about fifty yards down the road had received a severe wound in the arm and abdomen, from which she afterwards recovered. The assassins retreated southward from the field. It was a scene worthy of the gods to see these two young men facing two concealed assassins, and fighting them like men of iron. At one time, Monroe charged on óne of the villains, at the same time firing, and drove him out of the corner and forced him to take refuge behind a rail, which Monroe struck with a ball. Who can read this without wishing a thousand times that he had shot the life's blood out of his black heart! David was carried home by a host of friends, who had gathered at the scene. At the gate he asked: "Is it a dream? is it a dream?" and each broken word gurgled up out of the red fountain of his life. His brothers were standing around, their faces sealed with the death seal of inexpressible suffering, and their hearts hushed in the pulsation of woes. His mother lay trembling against the casement, her heart throbbing with its burden of sorrow, while the issues of life or death were being waged in the soul of her son. His sisters were standing in the vortex of misery, praying for the dreadful slaughter to be stopped, and suing for happiness with the sunny side of life in view, Convulsive sensations of horror and afright, and smothered execrations pervaded the men, and audible sobbings and screams, with tears, were heard among the women.

This was the worst murder of them all. No other equals it in heinousness. You may combine corruption, debauchery and all the forms of degredation known to inventive genius of man, and cord them together with strings drawn from maiden's hearts, and paint the scene in human blood bespangled with broken vows and seared consciences, and still it will redden Heaven with revengeful blush and leave you blacken hell to make it equal. It had not been long since the flash of fire from the gun of his father's assassin had sent a blasphemous challenge to his life. The echo from the gun had not ceased to ring, when this deed of barbarity was committed. David was a gentleman in the fullest sense. There was nothing mean in his appearance or conduct. Twenty-five years of age, tall, and of magnificent appearance, and respected by everybody for his still, quiet manners. But on the morning of the 28th, the twilight shadow of death, cold and gray, came stealing on him. A supernatural lustre lighted up his eye, and illuminated the gathering darkness. At length his eyes closed, and an expression of ineffable placidity settled on his palid lips, and he was no more. He was taken to Tennessee, where his father had been, and buried. The night David was killed, the assassins had probably four stands, and there were no less than seven men on the watch for him; but after he was shot, he charged Thomas Russell and David Pleasant of being his murderers. Jordan Halstead and Samuel R. Crain came to Marion that night, and I wrote out the writs for their arrest; but it was near daylight when the *posse comitatus*, headed by Constable J. V. Grider, surrounded the residence of Jefferson Russell. Thomas was arrested, and a party sent on into Jackson County after Pleasant. They were both brought to Marion, and Russell employed me for his counsel. While he and Pleasant were in my office, Gordon Clifford, *alias* "Texas Jack," came in, talked a few words with Russell, and soon left town. Pleasant was about twenty-two. tall, awkwardly built, nervous, and seemed badly frightened. The case against him was nolled, and he immediately left the country. Most people believed him to be guilty. One thing I do know, that he was uneasy as an eel on a hook, and his confused behavior makes it reasonable to suppose him guilty. It is not my business to say who is guilty, and who is not; but, if he is, until repentence composes his mind, he will be a stranger to peace. Russell changed the venue in his case from W. N. Mitchell, J. P., to Geo. W. Young, J. P. All the batteries of the Bulliners were leveled on Russell. They employed three attorneys to assist the State's Attorney. W. W. Cemens was then employed by Russell to assist in his defense. The case went to trial on Thursday, but was nollied by The People, who already had another warrant for his arrest issued by George F. Crain, J. P. The State"s Attorney, Jennings,

had lost confidence in Young. In fact, being
a most consummate scoundrel himself, he
could see no virtue in anybody.

The object of the prosecution was to get
time to hunt up evidence; but it was a
source of positive relief to the defense to
have the *nolle* entered. I knew, most certainly knew, that Young would send my cli-
ent to jail; but now I told him for the first
time that we could clear him. The venue
was again changed from Crain, J. P., to William Stover, J. P., of Eight Mile, who came
to Marion and heard the case. The trial commenced Friday morning, March 31, 1874.
The Bulliners in Tennessee had not only said
that "they did not want any more Bulliners
brought down there in boxes," but David,
Sen., had come up to see that the guilty were
prosecuted. Tom's gun was sent for, and the
contents extracted. The People proved by
two witnesses that Russell was at the window
of the church that night, and the wadding
picked up from the ground where the shooting was done, was placed to that drawn from
the gun, and gave, as they claimed, an unbroken account of the St. Louis tobacco market. Balls and cut wadds picked up were
similar to those in the gun. They also proved threats. David's dying declaration, saying that it was Russell, was introduced. The
defense was an *alibi*, five witnesses swearing

that he retired at eight o'clock, was seen by them at half-past eight, and again at ten, in his room; the murder having occurred at half-past nine o'clock, two miles away. The tracks were proven to be two numbers too large. The prosecution claimed that defendant's witnesses swore falsely; but I said then, and repeat it now, that they swore the truth. When Russell first employed me, I asked him to call up his witnesses and let's see if they were going to swear harmoniously, and if there were any of them *whose* evidence would damage us, we could leave them off.

He said:

"Call them as you please; they will swear that I was at home. They know that I was at home, and you can call them on the stand without any drilling. I am not afraid for you to do this."

So, I say, if Thomas Russell is guilty, he came out of his window on to the stoop, and down to the ground, and returned the same way.

The prosecution was badly managed. One of defendant's witnesses was Miss Hope Russell, a sister of the defendant, and a lady whose exalted virtues and transcendent beauty claim a consecrated place in this volume. One of The People's witnesses was Miss Amanda Bulliner, both about sixteen

years old.  She took the stand with a helpless and confiding look, her voice was a little softened by emotion, her  rose-left  ups
curled delicately, but soon her clear, trans-
lucent eye lit up with a brilliant lustre.  The
shadows of misery seemed to depart.   Her
soft, round  cheek  dimpled  and  dimpled
again, like the play waters in the sun, in  a
lovely and touch assembly of charms.   Her
features  were  of  classic regularity.  Her
presence seemed to shadow the place.    So
pure, so truthful, so charming her  actions,
that all pronounced her a most gentle,  and
most noble creature.   Though never a jew-
eled wreath may span the curls of her bea-
tiful brow, yet, happiness may as well erect
its shrine around her, for Nature can no further gifts bestow.   Monroe Bulliner  swore
that he was within a few feet  of the assassins, but did not recognize them.  This was
a remarkable exhibition of veracity.    He
might have identified the parties,  and  the
world believed it true; but, firm as a rock,
like a sainted martyr, he stood by the open,
bold and honest truth.

One of the witnesses was the  famous
Sarah Stocks, who swore to threats.  Her
contour is not as faultless as a Greek  god-
dess, but her form and features had caught
some new grace from the times.  Her eye
was as clear and cold as a stalactite of Ca-

pri. She wore a sigh, and there is something
in a sigh for everybody. But I will throw
no shadow over her, for life in her is as mysterious as in the rich 'belle; and when   the
golden chariot of destiny rolls through   the
skies, she may take her   seat   among   the
great. On Saturday evening, the sun went
down behind a fleecy cloud, and kindled   a
volcano for   whose   silver-rimmed   crater
fiery rays of scarlet shot up the clear   blue
dome of heaven, and the lurid lava streamed
downward through vapor cliffs and gorges.
Alarm took the place of anxiety. The Russells, Hendersons, Sisneys and their friends
were in town, and rumor was rife that they
had a load of arms, and that they would rescue Russell if he was committed.   The people were scared, and went home. The State's
Attorney ran off.   The defense thought that
the Bulliners were going to assassinate Rus-
sel, if he was turned loose.   On   the   contrary, they had no such notion, but thought
that they would be killed.   The excitement
arose from mutual misapprehensions . The
sheriff   summoned   twenty-five men,   with
guns to hold the prisoner.   Calvert closed
for The People, amidst the greatest excitement, and the Court said the defendant was
not guilty.

The surprised   audience   looked   blank
and sad.  James Henderson and a dozen oth-

ers rushed to the defendant, gave him a pistol and rushed him downstairs, where horses were in waiting. Russell and three others mounted, and left town at full speed. A letter was sent from the State Attorney of Jackson County, by James Conner, to the Sheriff, to hold Russell for the murder of George Bulliner, but, for some reason, was not delivered to the Sheriff until he was gone. The hue and cry was levied immediately, and several days were spent in trying to find him, but he has never been arrested. The Bulliners offered $500 reward for his arrest, and $2,000 for the conviction of him and Pleasant, which they afterward withdrew.

I will relate one incident as an illustration of the excitable foolery of the times. One evening, when all hopes of Russell's recapture were lost, John Russell came into town to see Clemens and myself on business. We had a social meeting appointed at G. L. Owen's that night, for some days before. After Russell was talking to us, we got a buggy and started out. Going on, I told Clemens that the people would think from the fact that Russell was there, that we were going out to see Thomas, and we had better drive rapidly and conceal our buggy, and have some fun; which we did. Sure enough, here they come; on hand cars, horseback, and on foot, with general orders to arrest the "whole boiling," and put them in jail. Several hours were spent by these fellows in fruitless chase after "all three of them." There were several men in the raid, but I have never been able to find one of them.

If Thomas Russell is guilty, it may be that the almighty sovereignty, love, was too strong for him, and envy seized him, and John and not Davis was the one he wanted to kill. If he could have wrung this lady from John Bulliner, and unstained her life, I doubt not if the shadow of his own would not have again darkened it; and inasmuch as he did not, it may be that the arrowy words wrung by the hand of passion from each of them were destined to hang quivering in memory's core till they festered and bled, making an irremedial wound, shaped in the red-hot forge of jealousy, and cured only by the exultant feelings of gratified revenge. These little bubbles of joy that jet up from the tumultuous waters of passion, soon evaporate, and leave but mingled dross and shame to fester and canker the mind of its possessor, who ever after leads a life of infamy and its accompanying wretchedness. Whoever committed the murders is the guiltiest of them all. It was he who with death first knocked at our portals, and with buck and ball opened the flood gates of misery, and let murder rush with living tide upon our people. And today his life is ruined, his hopes blasted, and sooner or later he will come to sorrow, shame and beggary, and have the scorpion thongs of conscience lashing his guilty bosom as he promenades the sidewalks of destiny.

Thomas J. Russell was born February 1st, 1851, is of fine form, dark complexion, black hair and very intelligent. The charge brought no blush to his cheek, but throughout the trial he sat contented with but little to say, and kept watching the Bulliners with implacable glance. John Bulliner had his gun. In speaking of these troubles, it looks like repeating the old story, and opening the wounds to bleed afresh; but the cry of murder and bloodshed is of too common occurrence in this county, not to have it recorded. The smoke from one of these bloody acts scarcely settled on the field, when it was renewed. The report started and went the rounds, only to return and be renewed by the slaughter of another victim.

I am bound to record these acts as they have occurred, for it is a page of history, recorded and sealed by the blood of our fellow men, that will leave a crimson stain on the county, that will be gazed upon and wondered at by our young, years to come. The

Bulliner boys appealed to the law. They appealed to humanity. They and their friends rode night and day, and spent hundreds of dollars in prosecuting assassins, as they believed, but they were defeated. The law was not supported by a pure public sentiment of the people. The ones that they looked upon as being guilty were turned loose. What could they do? Must they be driven to the bushes by this hard bargain, or be placed for a lifetime at the mercy of the assassins, with their hearts enclosed in palisades of sorrow? They saw their father and brother shot down by vandal hands, and their own lives threatened by fiends stalking in midnight darkness. Is it a wonder that the spirit of retaliation seized them, and the stern old Mosaic law of an eye for an eye and a tooth for a tooth, went into full force among them, and they became aggressors themselves? Retaliation was taught them by every cord in human nature. They were drawn upon by every principle that calls forth human action. Their lives were a constant appeal to chivalry. What could they do but pick up the gauntlet hurled into their faces, and give vent to an anger long pent up? At this time there were interests more sacred to the Bulliners than those of peace. Justice was more. Honor was more.

—F 11

Fidelity to the memory of a murdered father and brother are considerations for which
those who spoke so loud in favor  of peace,
would have foregone progress and prosperity, and drawn the shot-gun in stern resentment and punishment of those who invaded
and violated their sacred rights.  When  can
son forget his father?  When  did passion
and crime ever estrange one from the other?
When ocean surrenders up her water, then
will the parents of his hopes and tears, and
the holy lessons learned on their knees, be
alienated from the son's heart.  They must,
if they are human, esteem revenge for their
wrongs as the most sacred inheritance.

The ordinary agents of the law had prov-
en insufficient, and Nature rose up to avenge
the injustice.  Embassadors were at an end.
Words of menace and expostulation  were
exchanged for the thunders of the shot gun.
The quarrels which a hallow place held in
abeyance were to be settled in the bushes.
The die was cast.  The god of the bushes
had been invoked.  The red hand of murder
was raised.  The feuds which had so long
fermented  among the Vendetta, were rele-
gated to the arbitrament of the murderous
shot gun.  Already the lurid flames of the
midnight gun lit up the fair fields  of this
county.  Already the smoke hung  like  a

wreath over the fairest lands of Egypt, and death stalked with defiant tread over the county. The past was an index to the future. The cries of our future victims had already reached our ears. The Bulliners were not uncomplaining sacrifices. The voice of humanity had issued from the shades of their farm, it had been unheeded, and one of them has since been convicted of murder. Whether he is guilty or not is not my province to say, but to tell the facts the best I can, and let the world pass its judgment on his slaughtered family.

John Bulliner could have been actuated by but one principle of human action in going into this work of blood, and that was revenge. If any thing could be tolerated to plead in extenuation of palliation of crime, surely it could be urged in his case; but if he is guilty, I would place his crime at nothing less than murder. The assassin of his father were actuated by malice. Their deeds were committeed with no ingredients to assuage or cool; making them the most dastardly acts on record. The Crain boys were actuated by a very different motive to join in this work. That is, where the power to do wrong with impunity exists, the will is not long wanting. Whenever mankind sees a chance of doing wrong without ever being detected, they do not wait for a provocation. The best men will do wrong, and nothing but wrong, if you remove the fear of possible punishment. It is true that the fear of God restrains a small class. But generally this is but a temporary restraint, and is effective only when protected from strain. But strain it; take away the punishment the men inflict, open the gates of crime, and some of the best men will become the most consumate scoundrels in the land.

So it was with the Crains. They did not commence killing from an inherent love of killing, but because it was being done by others, and nobody punished. Hence, men have been heard to say: "I might as well make some money as anybody else."

After Russell's release, several parties formed themselves into fantastic models, and scouted the country. Ready to vie with each other in general follies, they started out 'by being ridiculous and ended by being vicious and criminal. One of these parties headed by Vince Hinchcliff, arrested Gordon Clifford alias "Texas Jack," down near the bloody grounds, and after treating him very badly, brought him to Marion, and just before daylight, had a mock trial before a J. P., the State's Attorney reading the law out a patent office report, and probably the

drunkest man in the crowd. "Jack" was put
in jail without law or evidence—the only
witness being "Smokey Joe," who had never
seen "Jack" before. "Texas Jack" was a
very mean man, but he ought to have been
tried as becomes ministers of justice in her
own sacred temple. He came into this county in 1873, and lived around promiscuously
for two years, offering gratuitous meanness
for his board. He was about twenty-five
years old, tall, slender, fine-looking fellow,
and a very fast young man generously, a
noisy ladies' man, and horse jockey. He lay
in jail until October, when he was indicted
for harboring "fugitives from justice,"
meaning Thomas Russell. He gave bond in
the sum of $500, and after having a couple
of rows with Hinchcliff for the treatment
he received from him he left the country. He
said he came from Kansas, and Vince wrote
there, and his character was very bad. When
he was arrested, the word "hanging" was
pretty freely used, and I would suggest that
if he ever take a mania for suicide and will
come back to this county, he may find somebody who will assist him off in a romantic
manner.

Some of their scouting parties talked
about hanging men; plans were laid in Marion; meetings were held; names given; the

leading men on the Russell-Henderson side
were to be hung; but they never could get
the executioners on the ground.    After the
Russell trial, James Henderson was waylaid.
He sat up many a night all night, watching
for the assassins, but his dogs barked  and
his mules brayed, every time  they  would
come near the house, as if to warn their master that assassins lurked in the bushes  and
they would run off.  One night he hitched
his mules out in the woods  to keep  them
from making a noise, so that he could kill
the assassins, but just before they got   up
that night in shooting distance of him, the
mules broke loose and came running  to the
house.   He worked in his field, surrounded
by a dense forest, with Granite and   little
Frank Jeffreys acting as guards for him.

On the morning of May 15, 1874, while
Frank was on watch, he said he saw something behind a pile of logs in the field. James
looked and said he guessed it was nothing.
In the afternoon, Granite had to help her
mother wash, and Frank was on guard alone.
About three o'clock he said he was lonesome
sitting up in the edge of the woods,  and
wanted to come down to his foster-father.
James, who had been building fence,  told
him to come, and he lay down with the boy.
Three assassins lay concealed  behind a pile

of logs, twenty-seven steps away. The dripping drab of a summer sky overhung the scene in pearly sails, and just when our people were looking for light out of darkness, to unmantle the smoldering folds of hatred, they fired on Henderson, who lay in his side, the balls taking effect in his back. He turned over on his face, and put his hand over his eyes while looking at them. One of them walked out from behind the logs and fired at him with a pistol, and struck him in the hand. They then ran off. He said right there, while his agonizing nature was vibrating in horrid suspense between life and death, that he recognized the assassins as James Norris, John Bulliner and Manuel or Monroe Bulliner. Thomas Wilson, a young man who was near by and saw the men, did not know them. Henderson was carried to his house, and lingered eight days before he died. When the news of the shooting reached Marion, but little concern was manifested. There was a disposition that so long as they kept even down on the "bloody ground" it was all right. One fellow cried out, "Thank God, they have got the old king bee at last." But such a sentiment was too shocking to float unrebuked on the air of Marion. We know what such sentiments have produced in other countries.

History tells the fateful tale. The terrible record is written in blood, and the world stands aghast when the book is opened. He was informed that a bunch of bones would be rammed into his face if he repeated the sentence.

There was no high-wrought, inflated tone about Henderson. No straining or twisting of style, but all was plain, simple, easy and natural. He was compelled to toil for the necessaries of life, and bravely bore the frettings and raspings of this cold, dull world. To his friends he was warm-hearted, candid, earnest and honest, and would risk his life for them at any time. To his enemies he was cautious, daring and dangerous. He was a man of but few words, but wore a mild, firm fearless look. He is gone! and the silver-dusted lilies and trailing willows will throw their flickering shadows over his grave, made green by the lichen-fingered touch of time forever. Soon after his death his wife became a lunatic, and died on the New Year day following. On Saturday, the next day, after Henderson was shot, Jaston Ditmore was plowing alone in his field, one mile west of Henderson's, and about ten o'clock he was fired on three times in rapid succession, five of the balls striking him, one in the breast, one in each arm, one in the side and thigh; but he soon recovered, and left the country. No reason for this shooting can be given, unless it was that he saw the assassins of Henderson. He was in no known way  connected with the Vendetta. When the inquest was held over Henderson, the Coroner issued his warrant for the arrest of John Bulliner and James Norris, but they ran at large until August 25th, 1874, when Deputy Sheriff W. J. Pulley arrested Bulliner at Crainville. He was kept under guard at Marion until September 3rd, when he was taken before Judge Crawford on  a writ of *habeas corpus*, and was admitted to bail in the sum of $3,000. In October  following they were both indicted for murder. Bulliner was put upon his trial,  and  had four witnesses from Tennessee, who  swore that he was there at the time, and he was acquitted by a jury.

Soon after Ditmore was shot, John Rod and one other man were riding beside a field, three miles northwest of Henderson's,  and two miles north of the  Eight Mile,  when they saw a man fall down in the weeds in the field. Thinking something had happened to him, Rod went over to see; when he got within ten feet of the man, he rose and fired on Rod, shooting him through  the thigh, and then scampered away.  It was rumored that this was Thomas Russell, but rumor had him everywhere, so there is no telling.

On Sunday morning, August 9th, 1874, George W. Sisney went out to his barn lot, and two assassins who lay concealed in the fence corner near by, snapped their guns at him four times, but being wet with the dew, they did not fire. He was shocked, and called to one of his boys to come to him, when the assassins rose and walked off, and he stood watching them for over two hundred yards. He did not tell who these parties were, but at the October term indicted Timothy Edward Cagle and James Norris, for an assault to murder him, claiming that they were the parties. Cagle is nineteen years old, an orphan boy, slim, awkward built, fair complexion, very pleasant and agreeable. He once had a difficulty with one of the Sisney boys. He worked for David Bulliner thirteen months, with James Norris. After he was indicted he went to New Orleans, but returned, and in March, 1875, gave himself up and lay in jail until September, when he went on trial. I had opened the case for the defense, when it was nolled on account of Sisney's death.

About this time rumor was afloat that Dr. Bentley, of Marion, had cut some balls out of John Sisney, supposed to have been

received when David Bulliner was killed.
On the 17th day of August, W. H. Bentley
published an affidavit, stating that he had
never cut any ball out of or known of any
being in any of the Sisneys, and that the rumor was false.   John Sisney was not believed to be guilty, but made a very convenient
scape goat for those who were.

During the month of August, "Field"
Henderson and Monroe Bulliner accidental-
ly met in Marion, and had a talk, and agreed
to meet at Carterville, and compromise and
have no more trouble.   Monroe said he
would get John, and "Field" said he would
get all the Hendersons, and meet him on a
set day.   "Field" saw the Hendersons, and
they said so far they had nothing to do with
the troubles, and were not going to have;
but "Field" went to Carterville by himself
on the day, and Monroe, John and Vincent
Hinchcliff met him.

Vince took him out to one side, and said,
" 'Field,' these boys did not kill your Uncle
Jim. I know they did not. All they want
is to be let alone. The next man that is killed, the last one of the Hendersons will be
killed or run out of the country. You fellows, by God, can't kill everybody.   The
people won't stand it."

"Field" said, "Don't say you fellows, I have had nothing to do with it."

Vince replied, "You are the only one of them that has any principle. Old Jim had but d——d few friends; I was one only through fear."

He said he had sent for the boys, two new shot guns, and they had not come, and that is why he knew they did not kill his uncle. Here Monroe and John come out, and John asked 'Field' where Sam Henderson was. "Field" said he did not know, that he was afraid to stay at home and work. John said:

Sam is in the bushes, and if my enemies do not come out and face me like men, I will go into them myself."

But they all agreed to be friends and have no further trouble. "Field" was to tell Sam that he could come home and go to work and that they were not to hurt him; but Sam never came home. This was the first time that "Field" knew that Vince was an enemy to him. He used to deer-drive with his uncle Jim, and he was astonished at his talk.

On Sunday, October 4th, 1874, Vincent Hinchcliff rode out north about a mile, to see a sick man. Coming back about noon, and two hundred and fifty yards from his

house, several ruffians had concealed themselves in a skirt of timber, on the east side
off the road, which had been fenced in, but
had grown up with small bushes.  They fired on him sixteen times, four shot guns and
twelve pistol shots.  He and  his  hrorse
were both shot dead on the spot.  Robert,
who started down at the first shot,  turned
the rise, and what a scene was there  to greet
his eyes!  What a radia of woe  surrounded
his heart! What a halo of shame! With  an
agonizing spirit he looked and saw  Vince
lying face downward on the cold earth, shot
to death by unerring missiles from the murderous shot gun.  And the bright sun looked
sorrowfully down, a silent witness to this
deed of unhuman butchery.   And  in  the
woods near by were heard the screams of joy
and fiendish yells of these ruffians, holding
a regular kickapoo  dar  dance  over  his
remains, while the smoke from their  guns
was ascending high up in the dome of day as
a signal to the surrounding country that another victim had been offered up. Who does
not wish that he could have cut fire-brands
from the flames of torment ,and with un-
sparing hand  scattered  them  relentlessly
through that forest? Humanity would have
directed the stroke, and civilization coun-
tenanced it.  Heaven  help  the  assassin

whose unsteady aim had left Vincent Hinchcliff uncrippled for he had arms  and  he
would have instantly wielded them with  a
dexterous hand, and unbarred the gates of
perdition for two hell-deserving assassins.
At two o'clock of that day two men blacked
were seen crossing a field three miles east
of Vince's, but were not recognized.  At the
October term, Fielding G., and Samuel Henderson were indicted for this murder.

On the night of the 12th day of December 1874, Captain Sisney and George Hindman, a young relative, were sitting near  a
window on the south side of Sisney's house,
playing dominoes, when an assassin  came
on the stoop in his sock  feet,  and  shot
through the window as Sisney.  About forty
shot struck him in the right arm, and carried away the muscle.  Hindman  was badly wounded in the neck and arm, from which
he recovered.  Sisney's arm withered away.
This was a random shot, fired into a family,
and the wickedest one ever fired  in  the
county. Marshall Crain  said  he  did  this
shooting, and that there was no one with
him.  But the tracks of four persons  were
seen next day, and the sock-footed  fellow
made leaps that would have strained Marshall Crain considerably.  At  the  April
Term, 1875, Timothy Cagle was indicted for

an assault to murder each of these parties;
but on what evidence I am unable to tell.
After Sisney's death, both cases were nolled.
Marshall Crain also said that about this
time he tried to kill Milton Black, who
had fought "Big Terry," and that he waylaid John Sisney, and came very near killing Worth Tippy, one day, believing him to
be Sisney.

On the first day of January, 1875,
"Field" Henderson was in Carterville, and
Monroe Bulliner went up to him and asked
him to explain why he had inquired of the
chamber maid at the McNeil House, where
he slept. "Field" said he had not done so.
Monroe then asked him to go to the girl and
see. "Field" said he would not go, for he
had not done so. Monroe said that he was
satisfied, but a crowd gathered around who
took "Field's" refusal to go see the girl as
evidence of guilt. Rough words were exchanged and revolvers drawn, and "Field"
commenced backing off. He displayed remarkable coolness and courage. Any other
man would have crouched like a spaniel at
their feet; or risen like a demon to confront
them; but he silently withdrew and boarded
the train. The crowd got on also. Monroe
came into the same car with him and they
talked the matter over, but the crowd was

barred up in the baggage car by the conductor, who stood in the door. The train ran a half mile to Crainville, where all parties got off, and "Field" came on to Marion. It afterwards turned out to be one of Bulliner's friends who inquired for his room, in order to get a pistol he had left there.     Monroe Bulliner, Wesley Council, J. M. McCarthy, Hugh McCarty and John Moore, were indicted for a riot, for this affray, and were tried at the November Term of the County Court, 1876, and acquitted. When "Field" arrived in Marion, he went to the residence of J. D. F. Jennings, State's Attorney, to see if he was indicted for the murder of Hinchcliff. Jennings told him he was 'but to keep out of the way until Court. "Field" went home, five miles north of Marion, and Jennings came running up town and told that "Field" had been there with three revolvers, and tried to kill him and "played thunder" generally. And he had the whole town in great excitement. It was published in the papers, and went the rounds, that "Field" Henderson, the famous outlaw and desperado, had tried to assassinate the State's Attorney for doing his duty. The truth is, he displayed no weapon, but acted as gentlemanly as a man could, to my certain knowledge. I was Henderson's counsel, and we followed Jennings' advice.

In February, the Deputy Sheriff and another man went out to arrest "Field," who, when he saw them, ran up stairs, and when they came in below he climbed down the stoop and started off through the field. They took after him and fired on him six times. He returned the fire three times. After his escape he went to Kentucky, where he remained two months, and in April, 1875, came back and gave himself up, and was admitted to bail on motion, on the 13th day, in the sum of $5,000, which he gave, and at the October Term we went to trial, and proved by fifteen good men that they saw him near a church at the very hour Hinchcliff was killed, twelve miles. And the State's Attorney, after this eveidence was in, entered a nolle.

During the summer of 1874, there was an organization of fifteen men, near Carriers Mills, in Saline county, who extended their operations into this county. They called themselves "Regulators," and dressed in disguise, and went around to set things in order. They did not injure any person, but simply notified those who they thought out of the line of domestic duty, and even in financial affairs to flank into line again. They

—F 12

generally gave the victim such a scare that he was willing to do anything to be in company by himself. Such a band is a disgrace to any civilized country; but no serious results or disparaging influence came from this one. Rumors were currently circulated of the good they were doing. Lazy, fellows took a scare, and blistered their hands at work; quarrelsome women turned to praying, and brutish husbands became as loving as Adonis, under the potent influence of this country clique. There was probably an organization of a more serious character in this county. Several men were taken out and whipped, and some ten or fifteen notified to leave the county. This was during the year 1874-5.

On the night of the 23rd of October, 1874, a party of twenty men in disguise visited the family of Henry D. Carter, in Northern Precinct, and ordered him to leave the county within forty days, whereupon a fight took place, and twenty-two balls were lodged in his house. In a few days fifty-two men met in arms at the County Line Church, in daylight, and ordered six of the Carters to leave the county. Mr. Carter wrote their names to the Governor, imploring protection. The Governor wrote to Jennings to enforce the law, and of course that ended it.

Several anonymous letters were written to editors, threatening them, during these two years; but if there were ever any regular Ku-klux in this county, outside of the band who hung Vancil, it was in 1875, in the west and southwest sides of the county, and a small band which probably included some members of the Vendetta.

After the death of Hinchcliff, consternation seized every mind; mutual distrust and a want of confidence was felt. The solemn pallor of cholera times hung over our people. Silence prevaded the air. The responsible men were seen standing around in groups, whispering questions that no man dare answer; while the irresponsible part, and dead-beats were lopping their horses about town, and making wild goose-sallies out to the edge of the bloody ground, quartering on some good farmer for a day and night, and then come back and report some long, airy story of the whereabouts of some noted assassin. Most men had a plan to advise, but the execution of it was generally left to reckless young men, or floating characters, who had nothing to lose and all to gain. Suppressed curses were sometimes whispered against the noted characters, and then the parties would be cautioned, lest he brought the killings to Marion. A low murmur or subdued excitement, would break out in the bloody ground late some evening, and produce the greatest commotion among the neighbors. Pistol shots had been heard at the back of somebody's field, and the sound of hurrying feet of horses running, and out would come five or six men, scared like rabbits, from a thicket. They did not like John Bulliner's movements, or Tom Russell had been seen, or James Norris, a desperate outlaw and daring desperado, armed to the teeth, was lurking in the bushes. Reporters for city papers would come down here, and go as near the bloody grounds as they felt disposed, find out what they could, (and in those days it was dangerous to seek to know more of the Vendetta than they chose to tell,) and then go back and call us a set of "blood-thirsty barbarians," "Italian brigands," and "Night Riding Ku-klux," and on top of these outrages a series of letters, signed "Big Pete of the Woods," were published by R. F. Brown, in the *Farmer's Advocate*, in Marion. threatening everybody and especially the State's Attorney. Brown's boy, afterwards, trying to convince me that C. H. Dennison wrote those letters, produced the manuscripts, and I recognized in each of them the hand-writing of J. D. F. Jennings, the

State's Attorney. He got terribly scared at his own shadow, and had the sympathy of many people in his great danger. And all the time he was fixing up a plan to steal something and run away, and make the people believe that he had to leave to save his life. He was so warm that he would burn a man with his kindness, and at the same time lived a life of cold-blooded rascality. He even reported that he saw men around his house, trying to kill him; but the people soon learned to take the square root of what he said for truth.

He was very popular, and the secret of it was his manners, saying and opinions. He was a professional doctor, lawyer, preacher, fiddler, horn-blower and a libertine. When he made music on the square, a crowd would swell around him. When he preached, they all went to hear him, from the talented aristocracy down to the boot-black. He was a rowdy among the rowdies, pious among the pious, Godless among the Godless, and a spooney among the women. He would get up in a sermon and rattle away until the shrouds and lanyards of conscience must have fairly quacked under the strains, and then go, get on a drunk. He was a clerical blackguard, whose groveling passions assumed full sway at all times. Lost to every

Christian restraint, degraded in his tastes, villianous in his nature, corrupt in his principles, how wretched was such an apology for a State's Attorney! He suddenly became wise and learned in the law about his compeers, and found out that all our witnesses were accomplicies without veracity, and those who were branded as criminals, looked upon the law with comtempt of judgment, and we stultified ourselves trying to enforce the law. "The wickedest of the people is indeed great, when the wickedest men among them are men of renown." And yet we had to look to a man as our leader in this great emergency, who bears the character of being a most consummate scoundrel. On his face was written legibly, " a liar, a hypocrite." A while before he left, he wrote a letter to Samuel Dunaway and a few other rich men of Marion, threatening to kill them, and signed it "Big Pete." Then he went to these parties and said he knew who it was wanting to kill them, and that if they would give him $5,000 he would hire men to kill them, and even told who he could get to do it. He was awful uneasy for them! But his insinuating toadyism and spaniel-like reverence for his "friends" were but idle and frivolous assertions in this case. They knew his warped and biased soul was steeped in infamy and falsehood. About the time

our people began to see the utter futility of
expecting anything like justice in a court
where this man was State's Attorney, he had
the good sense to defraud the county of
$900 and run away and owing everybody.
As a prosecutor, he was a regular sarcasm
on justice, a great hideous 'burlesque; free
from religious scruples, and ready to sail
from any point of the compass. He has gone
out to humbug some other people, and will
live in our history in an immortality of
shame and disgrace. He and Brown, of the
Farmer's Advocate, did more to injure our
county than all the shot guns in it.

In April 1875, the office was declared
vacant, and in June J. W. Hartwell was elected to fill the vacancy. On the 22nd day of
January, 1875, B. O. Jones, of Massac, introduced a bill in the Legislature to appro-
priate $10,000 for the relief of Williamson
County. But the speaker appointed a committee against us, with L. F. Plater, of Hardin, as chairman. He wrote to our State's
Attorney, Circuit Clerk, and others for information, but none of them ever answered
him, and the bill was cut down to $3,000, and
passed the House too late to be passed by
the Senate. Hon. A. C. Nelson, our Repres-
entative, won for himself the illustrious ap-
pellation of "Egyptian orator," fighting for
this bill.

During the spring of 1875, several
blinds were found near Bulliner's, and one
day John went to Carbondale, and a fresh
blind was put up north of his house, about
a quarter of a mile, so that they could kill
him, as he returned. Monroe found this
blind, and told John to look out, and thus
saved his life. At one time some men were
seen around the house; but they did not
get to kill anybody. At this time the people
were an entire army of observers. Every
man had his eyes riveted on the horizon of
crime, and his ears pricked to hear. On the
night of the 4th of July, somebody went to
Marshall Crain's house, in Crainville, while
he was gone from home, and fired a charge
of buck-shot promiscuously around his bed.
This gave Marshall such a scare that he determined to go back into the Vendetta, which
he had left in January, and he said he hired
to John Bulliner to kill Sisney for $300, and
got all the money but $5. He wanted to kill
John Sisney first, but Bulliner would have
him kill the old man. Being afraid to stay
at home, he and his wife went to Samuel
Music's to board. On the 7th he asked Sam,
if he got into trouble would he help him out.
Sam said he would. Again, on the 8th, he
asked him, and Sam said he would swear for
him, and clear him. Marshall said John Sis-

ney had shot into his house, and he wanted revenge, and he wanted Sam to swear him out of trouble. Sam agreed to do so.

About ten o'clock Wednesday, July the 28th, Marshall started out from Music's, and went to a neighbor's, and borrowed a gun, saying that he wanted to go a hunting; but in fact he hardly knew what he did want with it. He went down within two miles of Carbondale, and concealed his gun in an old house on the road, near Mrs. Snider's, and went into the field where the Snider boys were thashing wheat. Here he met the famous Allen Baker, and had a few words with him privately. This was late in the evening. He then went back to the old house and left his coat and boots, and just after dark, went to Carbondale, where George Sisney had moved a few months before for safety. It was raining, and in going up East Main street, he carried a board over his gun, to keep it dry. When he met anybody he would lay his gun under the side-walk, pass on and then go back and get it; and this he did as many as six times. Capt. Sisney lived on the northeast corner of the square, his house extending eastward and facing south, with a porch on the south side. Marshall went up slowly, but Sisney had already retired. He waited around the premises for a while, and when anybody would pass with lanterns, he would go back to an old wood shed in a dark alley, on the east side. The evening train was late that night, and when Marsh, had got tired and almost gave up all hope, it came, and on board was Overton Stanley, a friend of Sisney's, who went directly to Sisney's house to get Sisney to sign a note with him as his security. He called, and about half past nine o'clock, Sisney came down in his parlor, and after lighting a lamp, signed the note and sat down near a window, on the south side; his hands lay folded across his lap. It was a night of rain and clouds. The wind swept sighingly through the foliage of the trees, with a rustling sound, as of swollen waters. The long, plaintive howl of the watch dog came hurriedly by, and mournfully fell an the ears of Marshall Crain, when the sobs of the gale would subside. He went into the old shed and put fresh caps on his gun, and then went slipping, half stooped along on the    porch but was so thirsty that he laid his gun down and went out into the street and drank out of a mud-hole with his hands; then taking his gun, he stepped to the window. The curtains were blown about softly in the breeze. All inside wore the sombre gray tint of light. He gently blowed against the curtains, and saw two men, but could not tell which was Sisney. Again he blowed and saw a pair of legs, and was about to shoot, when he saw that the man had on fine boots. That was not Sisney. His breath, assisted by the wind, parted the curtains again, and he saw the black, stiff beard of Sisney. He stepped back, cocked both barrels of his gun, raised it to his shoulder. Just then he heard Sisney say, "I guess it is time to retire." Stanley asked,

"What kind of a man is George Moore?"

Sisney replied: "He is a bad one; he is all right, and is a worse man than he looks to be."

Marshall Crain pulled the trigger, and George W. Sisney laid still in death's eternal sleep. Marshall heard Sisney say—

"Oh, Lord, I am shot! Lord, have mercy on me!"

It was the only expression of despair that ever came from the brave heart of George Sisney, although he had four times before survived the murderous missiles.
"Wearied, forsaken and pursued, at last,
All safety in despair of safety placed,
Courage he thence resumes, resolves to bear
All their assaults, since 'tis in vain to fear."

After the murder that night, the winds sallied, and a cold, white fog laid its moist fingers on the heated pulse of Carbondale. The scene in this stricken, smitten and afflicted family was heart rending. Mrs. Sisney, who had raised the window up stairs and cried out for help, was now wringing her hands in agony. Martha Jane, who was sleeping in an adjoining room below, woke up, heard a strangling noise, and asked her father what was the matter; receiving no answer, dressed herself, and went into the parlor. The light, six feet away, had been blown out by the concussion, and all was dark. Stanley said—

"Your pa is shot. Mr. Sisney is killed dead."

He had locked the front door, and she opened it and called for help. The sad and heavy-hearted citizens came in droves, their eyes flashing with resentment, and their spirits rankling in bitter malice. They followed the assassin a piece but could not keep his trail. Sisney remained seated for an hour and a half upright in his chair, shot under the left nipple,which made a hole two inches in diameter. He was buried on the 30th, on his homestead, with Masonic honors. There we leave him forever. Shall his memory go back to oblivion and shame, or shall it follow those who have gone without blame from intelligence, virtue or Heaven?

I would write for his epitaph, "An honest, brave. true man."

After the murder, Marshall Crain ran down East street with his gun, and crossed into the bushes on the north side of the road leading east. When he got into Mrs. Snider's field, he got lost in the dark. The thunders bellowed over head like the trumpet of the great arch-angel calling sinners to judgment. Crash upon crash, and roar upon rcar, till the vast vault of heaven was filled with the giant sound. The lightning, broad and bright flooded the whole sky with a lurid red, flashing its fire across the field, and illuminating with a dreadful light his solitary form alone amid the wrath of the elements. After wading through swamps and bushes, he arrived at his mother-in-law's, nine miles from Carbondale, just before day, tired, wearied and almost broken down. Next morning, Colonel D. H. Bush, of Carbondale, offered a reward of $500, which he refused to pay on the conviction of Bulliner and Baker for the murder of Sisney, and suit was brought against him by B. F. Lowe, which is now pending. Samuel Music, who was teaming for Captain Landrum, was in Carbondale the day Sisney was killed. He saw Marshall Crain there (for he had been in a while that day), who told him that he

was there to kill Sisney, and he told Sam
where he had left his coat and boots. Sam
got them, and wore the boots out. On the
morning after the murder, Music said, he,
Marshall, and Allen Baker met in Carterville,
and Baker gave as a reason for not coming to
help him in the killing, as he had promised
at Mrs. Snider's, that it rained. About noon,
Marshall, Music and John Bulliner, met in
Crainville, and Marshall told John that Sam
was into this thing too, now, and they both
told Sam if he told this he would be the next
man killed. Marshall then told John how he
killed Sisney, and John paid him $15, and
told him he would pay him the rest when he
sold his wheat. The same day, "Big Jep"
Crain came to Marion. His presence in town
created a great deal of talk, and most people
believed he was in the Vendetta. He wanted to join a proposed company of militia,
and be the captain. He said he could stop
the killing; but before this a subscription
paper had been circulated to employ detectives, and he signed $25, and after a while
he said "he did not like the direction things
were taking," and withdrew it.

He went down to Crainville, Friday evening, about four o'clock, and he and Marshall
and Music (according to Music's statement),
went down to Marshall's old house, and after

playing cards and drinking a while, "Big
Jep" said: "The next man to kill is Spence,"
and told Music to go to John Bulliner's and
get a gun for "Black Bill" Crain. Music
said he would not do it; that he would be seen
but he would get one from John Ditmore, in
Crainville, if that would do. "Big Jep" said
it would do, and that he would go that night
and get "Black Bill" who lived four miles
south of Crainville, and meet him and Marsh
next morning at the back of Mrs. Hampton's
field, which is only three miles south.
"Big Jep" went off, and at dark, Music
went to John Ditmore's to get his gun, but
John would not let it out at night, and told
him to come in the morning, which he
did very early and got the gun, and put it in
Marsh's old house. Then Sam and Marsh
got three pints of whiskey, and met in the
woods at the back of "Yaller Bill's" field,
from where they walked to the back of Mrs.
Hampton's field. At the north-west corner
a path led up into the woods. They broke
weeds and bushes off and threw them in the
path as a "sign" and went on up the hill.
There they fired three pistol shots as a signal to "Big Jep" and "Black Bill," who came
about twelve o'clock, two hours after Marsh
and Sam had got there. The object of this
meeting was to initiate Sam into the Ku-Klux

as he said that "Big Jep" thought they had
better join them for protection, but they did
not do so. They agreed to kill Spence that
night. Sam, "Black Bill" and Marsh were to
do the killing, and "Big Jep" was to keep
them out of trouble. He told them, if they
got in jail not to mind staying there two or
three months, that the door would be smash-
ed in and they taken out.

They parted, and "Big Jep" went with
"Black Bill," and Sam and Marsh went to
Wesly Crain's and got dinner. Sam went
home and then to Carterville, and got some
more whisky, and at dark met "Black Bill"
and Marshall at the back of "Yaller Bill's"
field, near Crainville. They went up to
Marsh's old house, about two hundred yards
south of Spence's store, where they waited
until ten o'clock, when everything got still.
Then Marshall took a gun, which he had got
out of a hollow tree in the woods, said to be a
Bulliner gun, and   they   circled   around
through the woods and came up on the east
side of Spence's store.

The rose-flush of day had faded in the
West. The sombre-gray of twilight had fal-
len around them, and the watching stars
had taken their stand in the   conclave   up
above , like unhappy sentinels   doomed   to
keep watch over the infinity of the ocean.

Spence was asleep up stairs. They were environed by the intense stillness. The thought of murder rolled slowly through their minds, but still they did not relent. The eastern horizon was silvered by the rising moon, and looked like a huge mass of beryl whereon burned ruby flakes of vapor, guarded by the vestal stars above. The Sapphire arch overhead burned beautiful and mellow. Marshall went to the door and called out, "Mr. Spence." Spence asked who was there. Marshall said, "John Sisney; I want to get shrouding for a child." Spence said he would be down in a minute. Soon the tall, august form of William Spence, illuminated by a solitary light, was seen towering grandly between the counters. When he got to the door, Marshall fired both barrels into his abdomen—a charge of sixty buck-shot. Spence said, "Marsh, don't shoot me any more!" This was an address to humanity. It was a heart-rendering cry of distress from a soul in mortal strait. Such a cry ought not to go unheeded by a brother man; but Marsh run his arm through the broken pane in the door, and shot him with a pistol in the face, as he fell. He then punched a pane out of the glass front with his gun, and went into the house, and searched around through trunks and drawers for two or three minu-

—F 13

tes, when "Black Bill" called him out. He had an old empty pocket-book. They walked off east, along the railroad, half a mile, and then turned south into "Big Terry's" field, and came out into an old road, where Music asked, "What will I do if I am arrested?" "Black Bill" said, "Have me and Marsh sub-pœnaed, and we will swear you clear."

After the shooting of Henderson, no man ever understood that it was necessary to fly. They separated and went home. This occur-red July 31, 1875.

William Spence was but little known in this county. He came here a few years ago, but attended to his own business and said but little. He was a good man, strong, firm and dignified to stiffness; but was making money. His death left no orphan or widow to wail at his hearth-stone. Though about forty years of age, he was unmarried. Af-ter he was shot he laid in his store all night, and was not found until the holy hush of Sunday morning rested like a benediction on the scene. Sunday morning, Marsh and Music again met at the back of Mrs. Hamp-ton's field, and Marsh drew his revolver on Sam, and told him he believed he was a traitor, on account of some strange whist-ling he had heard, and if he did not find the whisky, which he had concealed the day before, he would kill him. While Sam was preparing a hurried absolution, he found the whisky, which saved his life. Marshall afterwards said he wished he had shot him; that he thought he was neglecting his duty.

On this same day, August 1st, Allen Baker, who lived on the dirt road, at the Crab Orchard Bridge in Jackson county, was fired on by an assassin, who mistook Baker's shadow on the window-blind for his body, and let in a charge of buck shot without killing anybody.

Music was coming back from the meetings at the back of Mrs. Hampton's field on Sunday afternoon, drunk, as usual, and a mile south of Crainville, he fell in with Carroll Wagoner and his wife, who were going home to Crainville. He got in the wagon with them, and the subject of the murder came up, when Music said, "Yes, we put the damned old scoundrel out of the way." Mrs. Wagoner of course knew that "we" meant Music, Marshall and "Big Jep." Late Monday evening following, Music, Marsh and "Yaller Bill" met in Crainville, near Landrum's Mills, and "Yaller Bill" said, "Did either of you boys get my jewelry?" Marsh said, "No." Bill said, "If anybody got his watch, it has his name in it, and they will be detected and pull hemp as sure as hell."

He then advised Marsh to take his wife to her mother's and leave the country, and told Sam to stop drinking, or he would leak it out. He said, "There is getting too many in this thing anyway."

This conversation is taken from Music's statement, and was denied by all the other boys. This is the only evidence of "Yaller Bill's" connection with the Vendetta. Our people do not believe he is guilty. They say that if he gave Marsh the advice spoken of by Music, that it is no more than any other brother would have done. Music went to Carbondale on Tuesday, and remained two weeks. While there, Marsh tried to get him out several times, but Sam was afraid and would not come. Marsh left in about a week after the murder and went to Missouri, and Sam went to Bird's Point, in the same state.

Never has there been a season of such universal consternation and anxiety among all sexes and ages and was in this county. It threatened us and our posterity with perpetual odium, and the very thought of having our county branded with lasting shame, filled us with living emotions of anger and fire. All felt that it was a time to summon every aid, both human and divine, and with the bayonets save our county. Political prejudices and feelings, which had entered largely into the animus of the Vendetta heretofore, were lost sight of in the duties of the hour. It was an understanding that Republicans sympathized with the Russell side, and the Democrats with the Bulliner side of the Vendetta; but now public considerations of a higher character attracted the attention of our people, and they rose above the trammels of political sympathies, and united as a band of honest freemen. No language that I can command can give adequate utterance to the feelings that it awakened in us, to hear of our friends being shot down like beasts. It was chafing to our hopes and gadding to our spirits. Many believed that we were standing on the threshold of a mighty convulsion, and they watched it with wonder and awe. Others prayed to that Being who sets liberty up and oppression down, to break the tornado that was hanging over us like a pall. Our lands went down in value one-third to one-half. The coal fields lay dormant. The fields of grain that were annually gathered on the west side of the county nearly failed. These were stubborn facts, known at home and read by thinking minds throughout the world. The name of Williamson county had become a hiss and by-word. Strangers shunned us like a serpent, and the sting was felt. Affairs were deplorable.

Ruffianism was rampant. Noted asassins were concealed in the thickets of the bloody ground. This was a daily talk, spoken out in thunder tones, that all understood. The air was filled with omens of disaster. Pass the street corners and the breath of murder was whispered in your face. Bold assassins stalked unbridled and unchecked. To bring these outlaws to justice was the universal desire of our people; but how to do it was a point that put to silence the entire country. The people were cussing the officers. Those who knew anything were afraid to tell it. Some were clamorous for public meetings, others for militia, and a few for rewards. Massac county was crying to us from the memory of her dead Vendetta; Missouri was pleading with us with her mangled hundreds, telling us to think of the gallows and the recollections that it suggested; the newspapers were holding a regular matinee over us, and sending a devastating storm of shot at our blood-stained county. There was no relying on internal strength. What was defective within was aggravated by what was bad from without. The abuse from without aggravated the evil influence within, which caused the banks of crime to overflow, and spread ruin and woe over the fairest lands of "Egypt." The minds which needed harden-

ing were relaxed. The hearts which needed
fortifying were dissolved. The passions
which needed cooling were irritated and dis-
qualified for considerate action.

At this crisis it was suggested that we
meet and pass resolutions that there had never been any crime committed in this county,
and straddle the "dark clouds that lowered
over our house" on some other county.

During this year the most malignant
falsehoods and slanders were hurled over the
country about this county, and were received
with implicit faith. At any other time they
would have returned to pay the inventor with
a vengeance. I raised my voice against these
outrages, and claimed that it was steel pens,
not shot-guns that were ruining the business
interests of our county. I knew that it was
not the falling into crime that would ruin us,
but the lying in it. And I did not extenuate
crime by apologizing for the inaction of our
people. I agreed that all collective crimes
were conceived in darkness and nursed in secret, and challenged the attention of men only
in their efforts and results, and that all our
people wanted was time. They would not
raise vigilance committees, as they were advised by the press, and go out to cutting and
shooting their fellow-men, like the cruel
Moors. Unexpected as was this deep display

of blood-thirsty feelings, the country ought
not to be surprised that our people were un-
prepared to meet it.  We live in an  age  of
surprise.  The events of 1875 show us that
it is impossible to count on what next week
will bring.  We never can outlive conspiracy
until men are taken by the hand instead of
the throat.  I did not pause to deny the
follies and crimes of individuals in the county
had lent plausibility to the maledictions then
rife upon us, but insisted that the whole ar-
cana of human ingenuity had been rifled to
find a plan to stop it, and that it  would  be
stopped by rewards.  The mills of the gods
ground slowly in our case, but they ground
well.  Some of the papers, in  speaking  of
this county, had the skull and cross-bones at
the head.  I thought that reporters could denounce crime without criminal and barbarous
outrages on a  community  of honest  men.
Some of them evinced a reckless disregard
for justice, fairness and truth, and spoke of
us with a venom and zest that argued  the
basest kind of demonstration, which called
for stern and outspoken rebuke from every
honest and virtuous man.  They tore down
the protection of our reputation—the bul-
wark of society—and left us defenseless in
the presence of malevolent villancy.

That anybody should delight in this kind

of moral piracy, and leave a community open
to the ravages of moral cormorants, is a
melancholy subject to think of.  God never
gave any man the right to poison the springs
of happiness in this way.  But it is unjust to
charge the country indiscriminately with this
crime.  There were some noble exceptions.
The Jonesboro Gazette and Illinois Journal
maintained a diginified course  towards  us
that was as commendable and just as it was
prudent and wise.  During the year 1874-5
this county had as good and trustworthy a
set of Justices and Constables as any in the
state,  and  all  offenses, except  assassi-
nations, were as effectually punished.

On the fourth day of August, 1875, Governor Beveridge wrote to our sheriff, offering to do all in his power to  relieve  the
county whenever the Sheriff throught proper to call on him.  At the  August  Special
Term, 1875, the County Commissioners  offered a reward of $1,000 for each of the mur-
derers of David Bulliner, James Henderson,
Vincent Hinchcliff and William Spence, and
on the 9th day of August, the Governor issued a proclamation offering $400 reward for
the arrest and conviction of each of the criminals referred to, and also for the murderers
of George W. Sisney and George Bulliner.
And on the 22nd of August,  the  Jackson

County Court offered $400 reward for the murderers of Sisney and Bulliner.

This was a gloomy period, but it was that gloom which preceded the dawn. It was the dark hour which ushered in the bright morning. Criminals leave gates open for detection. There are certain weak meshes in the network of develish texture. We are just looking forward to no distant day when the dark veil that concealed the festering crimes of the county should render asunder by a daring and skillful hand. It came. Mrs. Wagoner told her brother, James H. Duncan, of Marion, who the guilty parties were. Mr. Duncan is a man about thirty-six years old, very intelligent, firm as a rock, and a man of remarkable courage. He could not withhold his efforts in behalf of his suffering countrymen, while they were bleeding at every vein. In him, the people felt that they had a leader in whom they could trust. A man of discretion and nerve, and though for a long time he was not publicly known in the work, yet he was backing all the efforts and laid all the plans. A woman told who were guilty, but it took a man of iron to arrest and bring them to justice. Mr. Duncan stood up firmly on the side of the people throughout the prosecutions, and but for his discretion and assistance, we might today be

suffering the calamities of a Vendetta. He
went to a "friend" and told him he knew
who killed Spence, and he intended to have
them brought to justice, and he wanted some
man to execute his plans. His "friend" advised him to get Benjamin F. Lowe, of Marion. Lowe agreed to go into it. Sam Music
was the first man to be arrested. Lowe
went to Cairo and inquired at the postoffice
for a letter for Samuel Music; being told
that there was one, he told the postmaster not
to let anybody have it but Music in person.
Lowe then got the deputy sheriff, and about
an hour Samuel called for his letter and
was arrested. Lowe brought him to Marion
on the 10th day of September. No confidence was put in the move by the people,
and consequently no stir was made until
Music was taken before Young, J. P., and
asked time for trial. His case was set down
for hearing September 20th, and he sent to
jail. Two hours afterwards, through the influence of Captain Landrum, who promised
him protection, he sent for the Sheriff and
Circuit Clerk, and made a complete confession of killing Spence and Sisney, and implicated "Big Jep," "Black Bill," "Yaller
Bill," Samuel R. Crain, Marshall Crain, John
Bulliner and Allen Baker. Lowe then swore
out writs against these parties for murder,

and the Sheriff summoned a posse of twenty-five men and boarded the train for Crainvile seven miles west.

Here "Big Jep," Yaller Bill" and Samuel R. were arrested. The Sheriff then went with a few men to "Black Bill's" and arrested him, and another party went after John Bulliner, and they were all brought to Marion that night and put under guard. Lowe went on to Carbondale and got Crain, and went to DuQuoin after Allen Baker, who had moved up there awhile before. They found Baker at home, and Lowe said: "We want you to go to Marion for killing Spence." Baker made fun of the charge; he got very mad, and Lowe took down a revolver which was sticking in the wall. Baker said, "You damned thief, put that back or steal something else." Lowe said he would when it became necessary; that he would look around—that he thought he could find a Bulliner gun,—this was their pistol. Lowe said, "I have been told that you are a brave man and a powerful man, and that you just ate men whole; so don't be surprised if I act a little curious in your presence." Baker demanded their authority. Lowe told him to look at Bush and himself; they were the papers in the case. Lowe arrived in Marion with him next morning.

On Monday, the 13th, their case was called before John H. Reynolds, J. P., but by
agreement was set down for hearing on the
16th.  The prisoners were loosely guarded
around town for a few days, and the people
became indignant, and the Sheriff put them
in jail.  Music accused Bulliner, Baker and
Samuel R. Crain with the murder of Sisney,
in Jackson county.  Lowe went before Mur-
phy, J. P., in Murphysboro, and swore out a
writ for them there, and  Sheriff  Kimball
came over on the 15th, and took them over to
the Jackson jail, where they were  tried  on
the 22nd, Music testifying  against  them,
Samuel R. was released for want of evidence
against him, and the others committed. The
greatest excitement prevailed.  A  special
term of the County Court was convered, and
the State Attorney  empowered  to  employ
counsel to assist him.  He employed the Hon.
W. J. Allen and A. D. Duff, of Carbondale.
The employment of these men  produced a
revolution in public sentiment.  The  rich
men stepped to the front, and the bummers
stepped aside.  Landrum, Ogden,  Nelson,
Washburn, Ferrell, Herring, Harrison, Goodall, Campbell, Grider, Mitchell, Young, and
a host of others, who have stood up for the
right and breasted the world's dark tide for
the good of the county, came on the stage,

holding up one hand to save the innocent, and the other to crush the guilty. And our imagination which had been so used to scenes of blood, was now playing over the rope and gallows; and our ears, which had heard the shrieks of agonizing victims and the fierce yells of their savage slayers, were now saluted by the slogan of returning justice.

On Friday, September 16th, the case was called, the People proving the facts above detailed of the murder. The defense was an alibi, W. W. Clemens and J. B. Calvert appearing for the defendants. Two of the Jacks and two Craigs swore that "Black Bill" was eight miles away that fatal night. "Big Jep" proved his whereabouts by a dozen witnesses. Other minor facts were proven, and after a tedious examination of two days the Court committed all the defendants to jail, except Music, who never had any examination. Music said that Marshall had gone to his wife's aunt in Missouri. Lowe, then in order to find out where his wife's aunt lived in Missouri, had his mother-in-law subpoenaed as a witness against the boys before Reynolds. State Attorney Hartwell then told Mrs. Rich that he believed they were going to impeach her, as she had to swear for the People, and it would be necessary for him to know where her people lived, so as to be able

to meet them.  She said her sister lived in
Butler County, Mo., and was married to Ben
Lewis.  She was not used as a witness. Lowe
left Marion after the trial and went to Makanda, Jackson County, and at ten o'clock in
the night started out to the Smiths, in this
county, who were relatives of the Crains.
He found where Marshall's folks lived,  so
that he could shun them ,but it being nearly
daylight, he went back to Makanda, and laid
up all day.  Starting out again at night, he
soon found where Marshall and  his  wife
staid all night the night they left the county.
It was a half mile east of Makanda. Marshall
counted his money here, and said  he  had
enough to go to St. Louis, and then to his
uncle, Thomas Crain, in Boone County, Ark.
They left here two weeks before  for  St.
Louis, from where he went to Springfield,
and then to Boone County, Ark., but returned
to Butler County, Mo. He left his wife here
with Dr. Adams, and started on foot to the
Cherokee Bend to pick cotton, and had  got
sixty-five miles when he was arrested.

From Makanda, Lowe came to Marion,
and on September 20th left for Butler County, Mo.  On arriving there, he hired A. Thomas to go out to Dr. Adams and make a survey.  He found that Marshall had left  on
foot for the Bend, carrying a pistol, a budget,

and wearing velvet pants. The County Attorney wanted Lowe to remain there until
Marshall returned, saying that Dr. Adams
would report the fact; but Lowe left Thomas
to arrest him if he returned ,and took the
train for Corning, Ark., thirty-three miles.
Here he hired a constable, and left for the
Cherokee Bend. Fifteen miles from here he
struck Marshall's trail. He had traveled
through a wild, sunburnt, arid waste, whose
solemn silence is rarely ever broken by the
tread of a white man, and his tracks were
plainly to be seen in the sand, where the
thirsty earth gaped under the merciless sun.
Marshall had given his name as "Crain,"
from Missouri, and had tried to hire at every
place he came to. For fifteen miles Lowe
followed his trail. Marshall was inquiring
for Jacksonport, and Lowe, when asked what
he wanted with him, would say, "he stole a
watch up in Missouri." They came to a river,
when the ferryman told them that Crain was
at Mr. Gray's, a half mile ahead. They rode
on up to the house, and a woman was standing at the gate, and when asked said Marshall was in the house, with a chill on him.
It was a double log house, with a bed-room
between. Lowe went in, and Marshall was
lying fast asleep on the bed. Lowe gave him
a shake, and he awoke very suddenly, rais-

ed up and reached for his pistol over his head. Lowe pushed him back with a Derringer, and asked him his name. He said, "Marshall Crain," and asked, "who are you?" Lowe said, "You know me." Marsh said, "Yes, how are you, Frank Lowe?" The constable was at the foot of the bed. Lowe told him he had a warrant for his arrest, and asked him if he should read it. Marsh said, "No." Lowe then tied him, and took his pistol, and put him on horseback behind himself. At this juncture Gray came out of the field, and Lowe apologized for the liberty he had taken. Gray said it was all right.

The sun was half an hour high, and it was twelve miles to William Gossett's, the next house, where they arrived at ten o'clock. There they got supper. Frank then made a bed on the floor for Marsh, and hired a school teacher for $2.00, to guard him, and lay down himself. He saw Marsh untying the rope from his legs; he got it off. Frank rose and stopped him. Marsh said he would have jumped through the window and been gone in fifteen minutes. They started on, then, and arrived at Corning that evening. Marsh had a chill, and was put to bed in the hotel. Frank also had a chill. Marsh got something to eat, and then Frank called the jailer, and asked Marsh if he would go with-

—F 14

out a requisition; if he would not, he would
put him in jail and get one. Marsh said he
wanted the men to understand that he was
going to Illinois of his own free will.    He
was then handcuffed, and wanted Frank to
write to his wife, who was ten miles in the
country, that he was under arrest, going to
Illinois, and that she must not try to come
through on foot, but wait until she got money
from him. He said she would come through
on foot if he did not tell her. He said she was
too good for him, and he cared for nobody
else on earth.  Within four miles of Cairo,
Frank told him about the boys being in jail.
He did not believe it.  Frank  produced a
*Globe-Democrat* containing the proceedings
at their trial, which satisfied him.     Frank
said, "Bulliner, Baker and Music have employed me to catch you, so they could swear
it onto you, and then come  clear; that  was
the arrangement."

Marsh said, "I don't know so  damned
well; they are as guilty as I am in the thing."
They landed at Cairo Saturday, Sept. 28th,
at 4 o'clock a. m., and took a freight train for
Carbondale.  While going up,  Marsh  told
Frank the whole story that he afterwards
swore to.  On the train he was very  noisy,
hallooing for Jeff Davis, and talked freely of
killing men.  He was mad at everybody, and

wanted to be unhandcuffed to fight men who asked him questions. At one place, ten or twelve men stood looking at him. He said, "If your eyes were in dogs' heads there would be sheep killed tonight." Well might he be excited, for he was in the hands of a powerful, shrewd, ingenious man, who brought every cunning contrivance, and subtle influence to bear on him, to get a confession out of him. It was a wonderful achievement, on the part of Lowe, to get a full confession out of a great criminal like Marshall Crain in so short a time. He was afraid of a mob, at Carbondale, and seemed anxious and reckless. When the whistle blowed at Carbondale he was frightened. Frank told him that the good people and officers of Carbondale would assist him against a mob, and if he had thought of danger he would have telegraphed to Marion for twenty men. He wanted to know if the people were very bitter against him. Frank told him they would only hang him, that was all. He said he did not care for his life.

At Carbondale the people did not know him, but presently John Crain came in and settled the matter. Frank took him out to the old house where he had concealed his gun the night he killed Sisney, to get some powder and shot which he said Allen Baker had put there for him to kill Sisney with. They found the powder. Frank left him at Carbondale, where he received medical attention until Monday, when he was taken to the Murphysboro jail.

On the 17th day of September, Sheriff Norris wrote the Governor for arms and ammunition for a company of militia. On the 19th, the Governor promptly responded that he had sent 100 rifles by express. The sheriff also sent the names of Z. Hudgens for Captain, W. J. Pully first, and Wm. Hendrickson, for second Lieutenants, but these men were not commissioned. The guns arrived Saturday, the 21st, and an effort was made to raise a company of militia by the Sheriff which ended in a "big laugh." But on the 15th previous, W. N. Mitchell and J. W. Landrum returned from Springfield with power to raise two companies, which they did; one at Marion and one at Carterville. The company at Marion was raised on the 25th, and the guns opened. J. V. Grider was elected Captain, Wm. Hendrickson first and W. J. Pulley second Lieutenants. There was some opposition to the militia, but these officers were responsible, brave, cautious men, and did nothing to irritate the public, and went quietly along, doing their whole duty. The Carterville company elected Landrum Captain, Wm. Dowell first, and Wilshire Bandy second Lieutenants. A kind of local pride seized the surrounding counties at this time, and they were continually holding up the misfortunes of each other, and justifying themselves.

John Bulliner and Allen Baker were indicted at the October term of the Jackson Circuit Court and went to trial at the same term, defended by F. E. Albright, of Murphysboro. Marshall Crain, who was taken from his cell one night, made a desperate effort to escape by running from his guard and falling on the ground, but was recaptured. He had been before the grand jury and swore against Bulliner and Baker, but now formed the design of going back on what he had stated there, and clearing the boys; and wrote the following letter to them in jail, which he was probably persuaded to write:

"Allen, I want you and John to post-man Jack, Sam, Yaller and Thedford, Johnny Rich Jeff, Yaller Bill, Wesley and Sarah Rich that they were to have a surprise party at Sarah Rich's, and I came in eight or nine o'clock, on the night George Sisney was shot and that I was barefooted. I know I sent my boots and coat by Sam Music, but that won't convict me. Now, boys, do all you can for

me and I will do all in my power for you.
Employ the same lawyer for me that you
and Allen have got. All is right; if I hang,
I fear I will hang. John lecture for me in
this case and clear me. When Spence was
killed I was at Cal Craig's. Prove this by
him and other witnesses, tell to them that
I was there about half after nine o'clock, cn
the night Sisney was killed. Allen, you and
John and all the boys will come clear. I shall
swear that I was forced to swear what I did;
if I hang it's all right. I shall swear that
Sam Music told me that he killed Mr.
Spence, and he told me that he was going to
put ammunition in that house, so when he
turned State's evidence he could make some
proof. He told me this. Can you and John
state too that he told you that he put it there
when he was hauling for Landrum. If you
and John come clear, go and post Mrs. Rich
and Johnny, and Wesley and Anderson Thedford; tell Ant. Thedford to swear he seen
me close to his daddy's, at about nine o'clock
as he came from his daddy's.
He said he would swear anything for me. Post James Craig
and prove by these, and tell mother not to go
back on me, and clear me; they can do it.
Have they swore against me? Tell Jim
Craig I want to prove I was at his house by

him and another witness when Spence was killed. Give information how I will move my trial to Marion."

This letter was to be destroyed by the boys; but when Marsh went on the stand and denied as he was to, any knowledge of the killing of Sisney, Albright produced this letter, and asked him if he wrote it. Marsh saw the point to this, that he was to be made the guilty party, and he turned like a furious lion and swore them both to prison. Music also swore the facts heretofore detailed. The case closed on the 12th of October, after lasting a week. On the next day the jury brought in a verdict of guilty, with the penalty of twenty-five years in the State prison. The case was prosecuted by State's Attorney Pugh, and Duff and Allen, the latter of whom made the finest law speech probably ever made in the West. The prisoners were jovial and noisy until the verdict came in, when a sad, heavy, forlorn expression settled on the brow of Bulliner, never to be removed. Baker was evidently at his father's house, in Carbondale the night that Sisney was killed. He lived about two miles east of there, and went home about ten o'clock that night, and when arrested told Mrs. Hill, with whom he and his wife boarded, that his life depended on what she swore, and suggested that he came home about nine o'clock, but did not ask her to swear falsely. She swore to this conversation, and it ruined him. The powder and shot which they proved he bought, was probably left at Purdy's mill. He had had a difficulty with Purdy a while before. $200 worth of belts were cut to pieces, and some powder, shot and caps found lying there.

Baker is about thirty-three years old, fair complexion, long black hair, thin build, and has a desperate-looking gray eye; raised in this county. He was considered a wild reckless, uncertain fellow. He once killed a man near Pine Bluff, Arkansas, while a soldier, and was sentenced to six months' imprisonment in the military prison. He had been married for some months. Marshall Crain once said to me, "Milo, I have got religion as to all my sins but one, and I want to ask you about that." "What is it?" I asked. He answered, "You know I swore a lie against Allen Baker; it was me that killed Sisney, and I swore that it was him." I asked him why he did it. He said, "To save my own neck." I told him that I was no preacher, but if he acted in good faith to save his own neck, it was no sin, but I thought self-defense; that a man had a right to exert all the powers which God had given him, to save his neck, either to swear a lie or to take life. He said that was looking at it in a new light. I said, "Then, Marsh Baker is not guilty?" He replied, "Well—yes—God d— him; he got nothing but justice. He was always agreeing, promising and contracting, but I never could get him on the grounds."

It was a heart-rending scene to see John Bulliner parting from his aged mother. He went to the penitentiary and she returned home, to live through dark days and nights, with the clumsy and crude condolence this world gives, and now lives in a little cottage, a half-mile north of the Bulliner homestead. Her life speaks, and her children read in it, "No ray of light for the future." Henceforth she can say, "I'll bear affliction till it do cry out itself enough, enough, and die. The scene of beauty and delight is changed. No roses bloom upon her faded cheeks. No laughing graces, wanton in her eyes; but grief, lean-looking, sallow care and pining discontent; a rueful train dwells on her brow, all forlorn."

At the October session of the Williamson Circuit Court, Music, "Big Jep," "Black Bill," "Yaller Bill," and Marshall, were all indicted for the murder of Spence. Music's case was continued; Noah W. Crain alias "Yaller Bill," was admitted to bail on motion; William J. Crain alias "Big Jep,"

and William J. Crain alias "Black Bill"
prayed for a change of venue, and their case
was sent to Alexander Co. The indictment
against "Yaller Bill" was nolled at the April
term, 1876. On Tuesday, October 19, 1875,
Marshall T. Crain was arraigned and plead
not guilty. He had no attorney, and the
Court appointed W. W. Clemens, who filed
an affidavit for a continuance, which the
Judge said was not sufficient. On Wednesday, October 20th, the defendant again renewed his motion for a continuance. The
Judge said he could not entertain two mo-
tions for a continuance, but that every witness mentioned in the affidavit, should be
here tomorrow. The defendant then in person withdrew his plea of not guilty, and entered one of guilty to the crime of murder,
as charged. To this the State's Attorney objected, saying that he could not withdraw
his plea of not guilty. The defendant insisted by himself and counsel that he had a right
to plead guilty, and throw himself upon the
mercy of the Court. The Court then fully
explained to the defendant all his rights, and
the consequence of entering a plea of guilty;
when the defendant again, after a full knowledge of all his rights, entered a plea of guilty. The Court then again had the indictment
again read to the defendant, and then again

ask him if he was guilty or not, and the defendant again pleaded guilty to murder. The Court then ordered a jury called, when Crain said he did not want a jury, that he threw himself on the mercy of the Court. Then Judge Crawford ordered the plea of guilty to be entered, and the case continued until Thursday. On that day witnesses were called and examined and from the evidence it appeared beyond all doubt that Marshall Crain was guilty of murder.

During the examination of witnesses the court room became crowded with ladies and gentlemen. Marshall's wife came in and took a seat by him. She is a small, sallow, serene, calm-looking woman, with a half-closed, glassy, soulless eye. She seemed perfectly indifferent to the battery of eyes upon her. At the close of the evidence, Marshall, who had set like a statue, only occasionally laughing, seemed nervous and exicted. After a few minutes of awful suspense, Judge M. C. Crawford said:

"It is not often that we are called to decide a question of so great importance as this. Marshall Crain has been indicted, arraigned and now acknowledges himself guilty of the highest crime known to the law." Here he rehearsed the manner of his pleading guilty, and said, "it is natural for all men to avoid serious responsibility, and I would much rather his case had been tried by a jury; but the defendant persisted in his plea of guilty, and threw himself on the mercy of the Court; and that I might act advisedly, I had the witnesses summoned and brought to court to see if the plea was really true, as pleaded in his case; and it clearly appears, not only by the plea, but by the mouths of witnesses, that the defendant is guilty of murder. A murder that seldom occurs in any country, and among any people, a murder without passion. Out in the still woods, God's first temple, they coolly and deliberately planned to take the life of their fellow-man." Here the judge and the whole audience were bathed in tears. He then went over the circumstances of the killing in a feeling and touching manner, and continued, "The Legislature, in making the death penalty, clearly contemplated that there would cases arise which would deserve this penalty." Again he rehearsed the facts to see if they met the requirements of the highest penalty. "By the law we stand or fall. No other crime equals this in coolness, and by all the laws of God and man, this man has forfeited his life to the people of the state. The responsibility is a great one. I hope to God that never again will a court in a civilized country have this duty to do. Here

Judge Crawford 'burst out in a flood of tears, and after a short pause, dashed the tears from his eyes, his face lighted up with an unearthly radiance, he said, "The people and my position make it my duty to administer the law and promise its judgment, and before my God and my fellow-man, I must do my duty. What have you to say, Marshall Crain, why sentence of death shall not be pronounced against you?"

Marshall, with a chilled and torpid color, a cold moisture gleaming on his forehead, a severe and majestic expression in his eye, notably intensified by the strong language of Judge Crawford, rose, and in a clear voice said, "I have had no time to prepare for trial. I have been forced into trial. I have been indicted and tried (Two-and-a-half days) without time to consult a lawyer. I was dragged into this work by other parties. I had a higher power and influence over me. I could not resist. I don't think I have done enough to be hung for. Spence was harboring parties that were trying to kill me. I don't think I deserve hanging. I was influenced by John Bulliner, a man of good mind and education, and I am not a man of good mind, and no education."

Crawford said; "I am now about to pronounce against you the highest penalty of the

law, and in all probability the sentence will
be executed, and you will have to appear before a bar transcendently greater than this.
There remains but few powers that can give
you relief. The Chief Executive may interfere and commute your sentence or pardon
you, and the Supreme Court may reverse
your judgment; but it is my duty to tell you
that neither of these will likely be done.
Therefore, I warn you to make your peace
with God." Here he spoke of the consolation
of the Christian Religion, and said: "I will
call upon you, Marshall Crain, as a living
witness, that I have warned you to prepare
to meet your God," and continued: "The
sentence of the Court is that the defendant
be hanged by the neck until he is dead, within the walls of the prison in the town of Marion, County of Williamson and State of Illinois, on the 21st day of January, A. D. 1876,
between the hours of ten o'clock in the morning and two o'clock in the afternoon of the
same day. May God have mercy upon you."

As Crain was taken to the jail he boasted
to the guard that he would never shed a tear.
The next day, he asked permission to come
before judge Crawford and tell all he knew
about the bloody Vendetta. But he was sent
to the grand jury and confessed the facts detailed by Music, as to himself; but was taken

from there, screaming at the top of his voice, and his atoning lamentations were heard around the jail for several days. The same day he wrote a letter to Crawford, telling him he had done his duty, and he hoped he would continue to do it, and that the people would forgive him for his crimes, and that the county might be restored to its original peace and prosperity.

After the same term of Court, Calvin Craig, Robert Craig, Monroe Jack and John Jack was indicted for perjury for swearing the alibi for "Black Bill," before Reynolds, J. P.

After the sentence of Crain, a guard of ten men were detailed from the militia to guard the jail by night and two by day. This guard did its duty faithfully until after the execution. Nightly attacks were expected from the "Ku-klux," which were supposed to exist in the county. The guards were often summoned to fall into line at some apparent alarm.

Noah E. Norris, the Sheriff, is about thirty-five years old, a quiet, honest man, and a cousin to the Crains, and on this account there was considerable feeling against him. He was often threatened, and violent outbreaks of passion were sometimes expected, and it was talked "that some man had to hang on the 21st." But it is true that he performed his duty, and that under the most trying circumstances and greatest disadvantages that ever a Sheriff did. When the feeling against him was at its ebb, he removed Charles Robinson, the jailer, a man that the people had confidence in, and put in David Coke, a comparative stranger. But it so happened that Coke was a man from the ground up, and made one of the best and most reliable jailers in the state.

On the 27th day of October, George W. Sisney, Jr., came to the cell, and Marshall said, "Wash, I am ruined, I murdered your father, and ask you to forgive me," and fell weeping on his knees. Wash said: "You murdered him without cause, and I will never forgive you," and walked away with the excitement of gratified vanity lighting with radiance on the vestal roses of his cheeks. Some said that Wash ought to have forgiven him, "that forgiveness is the odor that flowers breathe when trampled upon." Others said he did right.

Marshall spent his time reading the Bible until, by the 21st of November, he was ready for baptism, according to the rites of the Christian Church. He was dressed in a long, white robe, and taken out under a heavy guard, to the mill-pond of Mann & Edwards, and after a sermon by W. H. Boles, was paptised into the church.

November 27th, another militia company was organized in the east end of the county, with J. T. Cunningham as Captain, and George Burnett, first and John Davis second Lieutenants.

December 21st, when the night guards went on duty they went into Marshall's cell, where "Black Bill" and "Big Jep" also stayed, and Marsh was gone. The jail was instantly surrounded 'by the guards, who cocked their guns to shoot him off the roof. The Captain again went into the cell, and found that a hole had been sawed and burnt through the ceiling. A boy was sent up in the garret but could not find Marshall. The Captain then found him rolled up in a mattress, in the cell, having come down from the garret, when the alarm was given. He had commenced sawing the shingles out of the roof, and had his blankets torn up for a rope to let him down. How the saw got into the cell is not known. The other boys said they had nothing to do with the attempted escape; that they "aimed to saw out with the statute." After this Marshall was chained down, as he said, "for the slaughter."

On the 25th of December, James H. Duncan, assisted by W. M. Davis and J. V. Gri-

der, the plans having been previously arrang-
ed by Duncan—ran in on James Norris at
Mr. Poteete's, at a ball, five miles southeast
of Marion. This man is the most notorious
and dreaded of all the assassins. Sisney
tried for a year to have him arrested. He
was brought to Marion and put in the same
cell with Marshall.

"Big Jep" and "Black Bill" remained in
jail until the 31st day of December, when
they were taken to Cairo for trial. The case
was called January 28th, and lasted until the
8th day of February. In addition to the
facts detailed heretofore of the killing, two
witnesses swore to seeing "Black Bill" going
up to Crainville that fatal evening, another
that he was at home in bed next morning,
facts inconsistent with the alibi. Threats
were sworn to by Narcissa Waggoner on
"Big Jep" of a bad character. Music was
corroborated by many other circumstances,
such as the bringing in of the weed broken
at the back of Mrs. Hampton's field. Several other witnesses swore to the alibi of both
boys. A great many swore they would not
believe Music on his oath, and they proved
good characters. In all, there were about
one hundred witnesses. Clemens, Calvert
and Linegar appeared for defendants, Allen
and Duff for the People. The jury found a

verdict of guilty, and ten of them being for
hanging and two for acquitting, they com-
promised on a term of twenty years.  When
the verdict was read, "Big Jep" cried; but
"Black Bill" remained unmoved.

On the 18th of February, a motion for a
new trial was overruled, and the prisoners
were taken to Joliet.

"Black Bill" stands six feet three inches
in height, drak skin, sharp features, gray
eyes, black hair and mustache, and very neat
in his dress, about thirty years old, and unmarried. "Big Jep" this thirty-five years old,
stands six feet one inch in height, a full,
round face, large head, light blue eyes, brown
hair, fair complexion, and, like Bill, dresses
neat.

Music said of "Big Jep:" "He did all the
planning, but he is a coward, and whenever
anything was to happen he would skulk to
some relative, and lay concealed like a cut-
throat until the crime was over,  and  then,
like a bird of ill-omen, his death-screech was
again heard."

Narcissa Waggoner, who swore against
"Big Jep," (she having boarded  him  and
Spence at the same time they had their dif-
ficulity) is a daughter of George Duncan, a
good citizen of this county, and wife of Carroll Waggoner.  She is about thirty years of

age, and is a woman of strong intellect. Her
testimony was clear, consistent and conclus-
ive. Before the trial at Cairo it was whispered around that her character for  truth
would be assailed. But persecuted, wounded,
bleeding, hunted-down Williamson  county
rose like a furious lion at the mention of this,
and insinuated that it would be considered an
assault on honor, an attempt at justice; and
the noise silenced. She is the lady who un-
locked the archives of secrecy and  let  the
light shine in. For a time she kept the signet
sealed in her own heart, but her spirit chafed
and her divine form wasted beneath the load.
It came to her in her dreams that she ought
to tell it. Honor was beating at her bosom.
The lives of future victims were pleading
with her. The wild winds wafted begging
from suffering women to her. All social life
demanded it. The moral sense of the civilized
world called on her to tell. Our lands had
depreciated three millions of dollars, and the
people were hopeless; but she put her finger
on the guilty party, and the  fountains  of
blood dried up; and the breast of every law-
loving citizen swelled with joy and pride at
the action of this heroic lady. Humanity
will not forget the generous woman  who,
though living among the criminals, dared to
take the proud rank of dignified resistance

to subordination, and spend the unbrought grace of her life saving her country, where man had failed. She lives in this emancipated, disenthralled county today, an illustration of her exalted womanhood, with the gratitude of her county.

On the 12th of January, 1876, Marshall constructed him a gun out of an old tin can, by rolling the tin around a stick and wrapping it with wire. He then took a large cartridge which Norris had, and when he was turned loose to exercise, went to the provision door and called Music, and told him he wanted him to look at that, as he wanted to show him a sign. He then put the gun in the door and struck the cartridge three times with a poker, but it did not fire. One of the guards told Sam he was going to shoot him, and Sam got away. Marshall said he did not expect to shoot Sam, but to shoot above his head and make him break his neck jerking back. On the 14th, when he lost all hopes of killing Music, he threw his gun out of the window. On the 15th, the following conversation took place between him and Robert Wallace, day guard. Marshall, looking out into the hall, asked:

"Is that the place?"

W.—"Yes."

"Where shall I stand?" said Marsh.

W.—"On a trap door."

M.—"I thought I would stand above it; will I fall through to the floor?"

W.—"You will drop four feet."

M.—"I want to drop six."

W.—"That would jerk your head off."

M.—"How will the gallows be fixed; will the post come up from below?"

W.—"No; it will be a frame fixed on the floor above."

M.—"Do you think God will pardon a man calling on him in the last moments?"

W.—"I can not tell."

M.—"I heard Sisney say when I shot him, 'Oh, Lord, have mercy on me.' The Bible says, 'He that calleth upon the Lord, he will pardon.' Do you think Sisney is in Heaven?"

W.—"I hope so."

M.—"So do I, and I wish he was."

Up to this time he had been jovial and funny, but now he said he had troubled the guards enough; he had something else to think about; that he would do no more to get out, and he hoped none of them thought hard of him.

On the 25th day of October he wrote to his cousin, Jesse Ragsdale, of Missouri, giving an account of his melancholy condition, and on the 16th he tried writing again. He wrote a letter to an abandoned woman in the

south cell of the jail, advising her to live a
life of virtue. This was a sensible letter.
He was now daily attended by ministers and
religious people, and by his faithful wife. On
the 18th and 19th, the gallows was erected by
Samuel S. Ireland, by cutting a hole in the
upper floor, three feet ten inches square, in
which he made a trap door, and erected two
posts with a cross beam, six and a half feet
from the trap door. On the morning of the
19th, Marshall awoke and screamed out, "Oh,
Lord, let me die easy!" and then prayed for
a while audibly. On the morning of the 21st,
he yearned to pour the balm of forgiveness
into the goaded bosom of Music. The strife
was over, and the battle lost, and the scars
of a wounded spirit were imprinted on his
face, as the lightning leaves its scathings,
and the storms of passion leave their deep
and blasted traces on the soul. He asked for
Sam to be brought into his cell; but Sam
would not go. Marsh told them to get me,
that I could bring him in. Sam
said if I advised him he would go
in. I did not , but offered him
protection, he did not go. Marsh said, "Tell
Sam to forgive me." I did so, but Sam
would not, saying that Marsh had told things
on him that were not true. Marsh said that
was so, and now to ask him again. I did so,

and Sam forgave him for all wrongs. It was a sad scene—two desperate men tamed to child-like softness, and weeping bitterly. They then went over their troubles together, and I carried the words from one cell to the other. Soon after, Marsh's wife entered his cell, and he took her on his knees and embraced her. It was a scene which should be sacred from all intrusion. Even the eye of friendship should not invade its hallowed bounds. Her eyes glittered with a metallic gleam, and the soft curl of her lips was lost in a quiver of dispair. Her's was a deadly pallor. It was the incandescence, and not the flame of passion, that was burning in her inmost being. She would burst out into shrieks of great anguish, and then subside into sobs. She dreaded the heaving of her own bosom—dreaded the future and the world. If she could have died she would have been happy and holy in the hope of mercy. To be torn from a love made holier by past sorrows, was an insult to the attribute of Heaven. Marsh was in his sock feet, with a pair of jeans pants on, and a ragged jeans coat. He looked care-worn, and shed a few tears. Twenty-seven years old, spare-made, weight 120 pounds, light hair, fair skin, light-gray eyes, with a bashful expression. He was married to Miss Rhoda Rich, March 4th,

1874. In speaking of the murder of James Henderson, Marshall said that John Bulliner gave Jonas G. Ellett and Mart. Dyal $300 to do it.

By ten o'clock an anxious and expectant crowd was swaying to and fro in front of the jail. He bade farewell to his friends, and told them to bury him in the Hampton Cemetery. At eleven o'clock the militia formed on the square, and marched to the jail and surrounded it. At least 3,000 people were present. The jail is situated a little southeast of the Square, and is a brick building, two stories high, with the cells up stairs. At twelve o'clock he was dressed in a white suit, with his robe over it. At twelve o'clock and ten minute he took his leave of his wife. At twelve o'clock and twenty minutes, with a firm step, he walked out of the cell and stood before a window on the east side, and in a strong voice said: "Gentleman, I must make a statement in regard to this matter. I feel it my duty to God and man to make it. I am guilty of killing the two men. My punishment is just. I hope all of you will forgive me. I pray God will judge and prosper this country. Good-bye to all." He then read a poem of twenty-four verses, which he composed for the occasion. Then, with a firm, steady step, he walked on to the trap-

door.   At 12:34 Sanford W. Gee read a few
passages of Scripture from John, and then
sung, "There is a fountain filled with blood,"
Crain and all the rest joining in the singing,
and then Gee prayed, Crain getting on his
knees.  The jury was then called and answered.  About thirty persons were in  the
hall.  At 12:46 his  legs and  arms  were
bound; at 12:52 the white cap was put on
his head, and John  B.  Edrington, Deputy
Sheriff, who told him that he had a death
warrant, saying,  at  this hour and at this
place he was ordered to hang him.  At 12:54
the rope was put on his neck, and the  front
part of the cap pulled down by J. L. Kelly.
When he was asked if he had anything to
say, said, "I am the murderer of  William
Spence and George Sisney; that is all I have
to say." He was asked if he was ready to receive the execution, and said, "I am."   He
was then told that he had four minutes to live
and said, "That was all." At 12:56 the Deputy said, "Time up," and Brice Holland sev-
ered the rope which held the trap-door,  and
Marshall Crain swung between Heaven and
earth.  After the jerking of the rope   he
swung around and then was still; he did not
struggle.  At 1:06 his pulse beat twenty; at
1:18 no pulsation at his wrist; at 1:22 pulsation ceased, and life was pronounced ex-

tinct by Drs. S. H. Bundy and John O'Hara.
After hanging thirty minutes the body was
cut down, and his neck was found partially
dislocated; the eyes and countenance looked
natural. Sheriff Norris mournfully did his
duty up to the time of the execution and then
left, saying the law should take its course.
At 1:30 his body was put in a coffin and tak-
en outside the jail and exhibited to the people, and then given to 'brother Warren, who
started at 3:00, for home. He was buried
next day. And the wild winds of heaven will
sing their hoarse lullaby over his grave until the mighty angel Gabriel writes the solemn legend, "Finis," on the hoary page of
time.

No polished stela points to his rest. He
left to his wife as a legacy, the memory of a
sad and unhappy man. He had nothing to
plead in extenuation of his crime against
the laws of his country; but he has the frail-
ty of human nature to plead for him at the
bar of God. This is a plea that has ever
opened the chambers of mercy to the sorrow-
ing children of men. Crain was hung, "and
yet men whose guilt has wearied Heaven for
vengeance, are left to cumber earth." Marshall was not a man of genius; but when he
came to this work of blood his skill was displayed in a wonderful manner. So ingen-

iously were his plans laid, and so dexterously executed that nothing but treachery itself could unravel them.

Part of Marshall's poem was discovered by Cyrus O'berly to have been taken from one by William Delaney, a New York desperado.

James Norris is twenty-five years old, a large, fine-looking man, very intelligent and pleasant, but was a wild, reckless boy—loved all kinds of amusements, and got into some difficulties, and was several times indicted. His father is a respectable citizen of this county. James worked for Bulliner in 1874, when he got into the trouble with Russell and Pleasant. At the April term 1876, he was indicted for the murder of James Henderson, and went to trial defended by Clemens and myself—Allen and Duff prosecuting. Henderson's dying declaration was introduced, saying that he saw and knew Norris; also, Jacob Beard testified that he met Norris in Cairo, five days after the shooting, and Norris was armed, and said he was on the scout, and asked if Henderson was dead, saying he knew who killed him. The defense was an alibi, four witnesses swearing that he was in Tennessee that very day. The jury found him guilty, and fixed his time at eighteen years. In overruling the motion for a new trial, the Court said he could not let the verdict stand, only on the fact that Beard's testimony made him an accessory to the crime. He was carried to Joliet, April 27th. Since that Clemens went to McNairy county, Tennessee, and got fifteen other affidavits that he was there at the time.

It had been reported in Tennessee that some of the Hendersons were seen there trying to kill Norris and Bulliner, and a company of one hundred men were raised and scouted the country there, in which Norris took part; but the Governor refused to pardon him. The people said "This 'alibi' business is getting 'too thin'," and there was a strong prejudice existing here against the Bulliner family in Tennessee. They thought David Bulliner, Sr., was running the whole Bulliner side of the Vendetta, and any one coming from McNairy county was looked upon as a scoundrel. This was all wrong. David Bulliner is a good man, and his son George is as polished a gentleman as lives in Tennessee. Those other men are common, sober, honest men. James Norris was not proven guilty.

Samuel Music stands five feet ten inches high, thirty-four years old, spare built, light complexion, high cheek bones, pale blue eyes, moustache, and a low, broad forehead, with

black, curling hair, and has an honest, open
countenance. He was born in 1842, in Jefferson County, Illinois. He had three sisters
and four brothers. His father was a poor
farmer, and at ten years of age Sam lost his
mother. In 1854, his father moved to Union
County, Ky. When the war came up, he and
two of his brothers joined the 13th Kentucky
(rebel) Cavalry, and served one year. Was
in the battles of Fort Donelson, Uniontown
and Rollington. He deserted the rebels and
took the oath. In 1863, his father moved
back to this state. Sam came back and was
arrested and taken to Louisville, where he
remained three months, and was tried for being a guerrilla, and turned over as a prisoner
of war, and sent to Camp Chase. In 1865,
he was turned loose and came to Illinois.
He subsequently lived at Centralia, and for
the last eight years lived around Carbondale,
working, teaming generally, and drove a hack
to Marion for six months, in 1869. In 1872,
he hired to drive a log team at Mt. Carbon,
and, while at this business, in the edge of
Missouri, was married to Miss Mary A. Grif-
fan, a very handsome little lady. In August,
1874, he hired to Landrum to team, and
moved to Crainville. He has always been a
drunkard, and is illiterate. During all the
trial and fatigue of the prosecutions, he stood

up without murmur or complaint. His fortitude never failed under the most searching cross-examinations, but mild, firm and confiding, he told the same story over and over. If he had refused to testify, or had broken down, the blood of other men would have stained the soil of this county. He said he got into this thing when he was drunk, and had no idea of killing anybody, and now he had done more than justice, he had not been selfish from passion of princIple; but had told the whole truth. His case went to trial April 17th, 1876, defended by himself alone, Allen and Duff for the People, who proved his confession, etc.

The defense was that the confession was made under the influence of hope, and not proper evidence. After the argument, the jury took the case, and was out twenty-one hours, and failed to agree; eleven being for acquitting, and one for conviction. And the case was set down for trial on the 21st. By that time I was afraid to try to clear him again, lest I failed, and it poisoned the public mind against him. Thus far it had been his faithful friend, and the prosecution now threatened to be severe. So, the danger of turning public sentiment against him, was greater than the hope of clearing him. And, if I had failed, and the people turned against him, there would have been no hope of pardon. So, ⏋ was forced to agree to a verdict of guilty, and a term of fourteen years. Beveridge told B. F. Lowe and J. W. Landrum that what ever they wanted done with Music he would do. He, also, wrote to Duff ana Allen, when he employed them, that they might say to Music, if they thought best, that if he stood firmly by the truth throughout all the trials, he would 'be the subject of executive clemency. And the people supposed that he would make it a point of honor to keep this promise. A petition was sent him, signed by the parties designated, asking Music's pardon; but he refused to interfere in the case.

At the April term, Samuel R. Crain was indicted as accessory to the murder of Spence. He was arrested, but being in the last stages of a pulmonary disease, was bailed in the sum of $5,000.

Milton Baxter had been indicted for the murder of Hinchcliff, and he had been arrested and confined in jail a while. At this term the People nolled. He, nor his brother, were connected with the Vendetta, no further than being strong friends to Russell and "Texas Jack."

With this, I seal the volume, and turn my eyes away from the bloody acts of depraved men, hoping with all the fervor of which my soul is capable, that God will add no other plague to our county. Enough has been done, to teach the world that sorrow is the first result of ambition, malice or revenge. The first gun of the Vendetta that rang out in the air, betokened a coming storm, and since then crime's destiny and miseries' tale has been unfolded with the stencil plates of blood on the souls of men. Many have become bankrupt on the pathway to shame. The different phases of human life display with unmatched and unequaled clearness to our senses the great wrongs and sins to mankind, and when we, in the course of our lives and professions meet them, we are startled from our unusual composure, and always do take them for warning in the future. I wish they would not occur to attract our notice. I wish we could be spared the recital of such crimes, revealing, as they do, one after another the sins and depravity of society. But justice demands that the guilty should bear the reproach, and that the stain should be washed away from the innocent. And while a man has a right before God to protect his own life, he cannot become the aggressor without blame. It was not that spirit of barbarism which kills men in Kansas, that governed the Vendetta, but that spirit which fights

—F 16

duels in Louisiana. It was the knock-down style of the West, coming in contact with the code of the South. The men who killed Bulliner would have fought him a fist fight, but they would not fight a duel; and they knew that it was death to insult a Bulliner and then face him. So, they laid down all rules, and that is why the shooting commenced on the other side. It would never have commenced on the Bulliner side; and it is not to be wondered at if they accommodated themselves to this mode of fighting in the bushes.

The age of chivalry is gone, but it has left its traces on the hearts, and it may be that they chose to exercise it in a more murderous, but less public way. The chastenings of honor inspired both parties with courage, and mitigated their ferocity; for they did not rob or steal, but simply killed. Their common cause gave them unbridled and unfettered alliance, each acting in subordination to the other. They held secret meetings, where powder and lead was the toast, and where they rejoiced over the death of an enemy like a conquering gladiator in the Roman Coliseum, with the fire of revenge roasting in their eyes. And so deep-laid were their plans, that treachery alone succeeded where stratagem and ingenuity had failed. The judgments against these parties stand out resplendent with the light of noonday as a beacon of warning that they will be duplicated when even occasion requires it. At this time, but one side of the Vendetta had been punished. All on the other side have escaped.

Joseph W. Hartwell, the State's Attorney, served the people well in these prosecutions, and they have rewarded him by re-electing him. He was born in this county, and raised a poor boy. When the war came up, he joined the Thirty-First Regiment Illinois Volunteers, and was at the battles of Raymond, Champion Hill, Vicksburg, Kenesaw and Atlanta. July 21st, 1864, at Atlanta, his left arm was taken off by a twelve-pound howitzer ball. He came home March, 1865, and that fall was elected County Treasurer. He lived very hard, having a large family, and studied law under many disadvantages, but was admitted to the bar in December, 1866. In 1868 he was elected Circuit Clerk, and again ran in 1872, but was defeated. In 1874, he was elected Mayor of Marion and May 15th, 1875, elected State's Attorney.

The people owe a debt of gratitude to Benjamin F. Lowe, for his bravery, skill and firmness. He was born in Effingham county, in 1838, moved to Marion in 1850. He was raised a poor boy, and worked around promiscuously. During the war he went South to see the boys from this county there, and on returning was arrested as a spy, but after a month's confinement, escaped his guards, and went to Canada. But he was not a spy, only having brought some money and letters through the line for the friends of the boys. Since the war he has lived at Marion and Murphysboro, serving as City Marshal at both places. In 1866, he married Miss Letha McCowan, and is a fine looking man, tall, slim, black hair, whiskers, and dark complexion. He is very pleasant, witty and an agreeable, reliable man. He is a professionable gambler, and makes most of his money in that way; but he is a peaceable, sober, quiet man, and a man whom the people have great confidence in, in emergencies. He took hold of our troubles when it seemed like death to do so; but the people rallied in solid phalanx to his assistence.

All men agree that the man who coolly and deliberately takes the life of his fellowman is not fit to live, and the Judge or jury who lets such a man go unpunished richly deserves the wrathful condemnation of mankind. Yet, Judge Crawford assumed a responsibility that no Judge in our country ever before took, that of hanging a man who plead guilty. And when judges and juries take the responsibility of trying and punishing criminals like this, the law will become a terror to evil-doers.

The practice of carrying concealed weapons, which grew out of the war, and which led to so much bloodshed, will soon be ended if juries will convict the guilty parties. At the April term, 1876, twenty-two indictments for this offense were found.

Williamson county vindicated herself. She not only furnished the men to suppress crime, but she spent $13,032.79, besides jail fees. We are now beginning to have bright hopes of the future. Men of property would not come among us as long as the pistol and gun were used to redress wrongs, and men were allowed to go a "gunning" for human scalps. This has ceased in this county, and now if those editors who labored so hard to traduce our character and disgrace our county, will do as much to restore it, soon peace and prosperity will be printed on the mangled tape of our county, and soon that odium that hangs around our name, like clouds around a mountain, will disappear, and Williamson county will stand forth resplendent in the light of a new civilization, conspicious and honorable, and take the rank her sons and resources entitled her to.

## EXPENSES OF THE VENDETTA.

| | |
|---|---:|
| Expenses exclusive of Bailiffs and dieting prisoners.......... | $ 670.24 |
| Witnesses for foreign counties . | 1,523.55 |
| Guarding jail .. .. .......... | 2,991.00 |
| Rewards.................... | 4,000.00 |
| Attorney's fees .............. | 3,650.00 |
| Hanging Crain............... | 100.00 |
| Coffin and shrouding.......... | 38.00 |
| Scaffold ...... .... .... ... .. . | 10.00 |
| Clothing for "Big Jep" and "Black Bill" .................... | 50.00 |
| Total ............... ...| $13,032.79 |

### OF POLITICS.

Until 1818, the nearest court was held at Shawneetown, but our people had very little business in it, for, at that date, there were only one hundred and fifty souls in Franklin county. The records were kept at the residence of Moses Garrett, from 1818 to 1826. In 1820, Lemuel R. Harrison, surveyed the town of Frankfort, and in 1826 the court house was built. The first Sheriff of Franklin county was David W. Maxwell, and Samuel T. Russell, of this county, was his deputy, and collected the taxes for 1820 and 1821. Then followed Thomas J. Mansfield and John Crawford. After the division,

the Sheriffs of the county have been, John
D. Sanders, 1839; John M. Cunningham,
1842-44; Joel Huffstutler, 1846-48; John
Goodall, 1850; James Marks, 1852; Joel
Huffstutler, 1854; Jacob W. Sanders, 1856;
Richard T. McHenry, 1858; R. R. Hendrickson, 1860; Lewis Spencer, 1862; R. M. Allen,
1864; George W. Sisney, 1866; Hardin Goodall, 1868; A. N. Owen, 1870; Z. Hudgens,
1872; N. E. Norris, 1874; Wilson J. Caplinger, 1878.

The Collectors of this county were William Hindman, 1839; William Dillard, 1840;
James M. Furlong, 1841; John S. Tutton,
1842; Robert P. Erwin, 1843, after which
the office was united with the Sheriff's.

The County Judge were Simon Hubbard,
who held the office of County and Circuit
Clerk, County Judge, Master-in-Chancery,
and Recorder of Deeds, followed by W. A.
Denning and Samuel K. Casey. After the
division, W. H. Eubank, 1849; David Norman, 1855; I. M. Lewis, Jesse Bishop, J. M.
Spain, 1869; and now Bishop again.

The Commissioners have been, Cyrus
Campbell, Starling Hill, F. F. Duncan, Joab
Goodall, John T. Damron, R. L. Pully,
Thomas Scurlock, Thomas D. Davis, John
Brown, Jonathan Jimpson, William Hind-
man, Addison Reece, Bazzell Holland, John

H. Manier, M. S. Strike, C. M. Bidwell, R. H. Wise, James B. Roberts.

The first Circuit Court was held by Samuel D. Lockwood, followed by Browne and Hardin. After the division, Walter B. Scates, W. A. Denning, W. K. Parrish, Willis Allen, W. J. Allen, A. D. Duff, and now M. C. Crawford.

The People's Attorneys have been Samuel D. Marshall, and, after the division, W. H. Stickney, Willis Allen, W. A. Denning, S. S. Marshall, F. W. Rawlins, W. K. Parrish, John A. Logan, M. C. Crawford, E. V. Pierce, J. M. Clemison, C. N. Damron, F. M. Youngblood, J. B. Calvert, pro tem., J. D. F. Jennings, and now J. W. Hartwell.

The County Clerks have been John Bainbridge, 1839; John Hicks, 1840; Elijah McIntosh, 1841; Thomas Davis, 1841; A. P. Corder, 1843; John White, 1848; John H. White, 1852; John M. Cunningham, 1861; W. N. Mitchell, 1865; J. W. Samuels, 1869; W. H. Eubanks, 1873. The County Clerks did the probate business until 1849.

Circuit Clerks, John Lowden, 1849; G. W. Goddard, 1856; John M. Cunningham, 1861; J. W. Hartwell, 1868; C. H. Dennison, 1872, and M. S. Strike, 1876.

In an early day taxation was no burden to the people, being only twenty-five cents on the hundred dollars' worth of property. Wolf scalps were as good as county orders. For the purpose of paying a premium of one dollar per scalp for wolves, an assessment of two dollars on each voter was made, but wolf scalps, bear, deer and coon skins could be exchanged for tax receipts.

It is common for us to speak of those early settlers as virtuous, honorable and upright men; but they sometimes committed crimes, and occasionally a man was sent to prison. The law was not enforced then, as at present. The people had an inherent sense of right, which was as efficacious in suppressing crime as the law. Hezekiah Garrett once killed a man in Frankfort with his fist, and was sentenced to the State's prison for one hour. He was a very good man. Most cases were tried by Justices of the Peace, of whom many ridiculous stories are told.

The county being mostly settled by people from Tennesee, in Jackson's times, they were all strong Jackson men, or Democrats; but after the slavery question was settled, in 1818, political excitement did not run high here until the election of James K. Polk, described hereafter.

The manner of voting was by word of

mouth, until 1849, when the ballot was adopted.

The militia was well organized, and kept up regular muster until 1845.   Company musters were held at David Norman's, John Snider's, Sarahsville, Thos. Hill's, Solon Sanders and Bainbridge.   Batallion drills were held at David Norman's, John Sander's, and Bainbridge. Regimental musters were held yearly at Frankfort, until the division, then at Marion, there being a regiment in  this county.   James Corder was the first Major from this county; Allen Bainbridge    was the first Colonel; John Davis, Brigadier General; John S. Tutton, last Colonel, and R. P. Erwin last Adjutant.   A great crowd  of these soldiers got into a difficulty at Bainbridge once, and just as they stripped  and walked out to fight, a streak of lightning struck a cotton-wood tree, near by, bursting it into splinters, and they all ran off like devils.

In 1832, when the Black Hawk war began, the Governor called for 230 men from Franklin county, and one  company  commanded by Jeff Stephens, went from Franklin county, and the others from what is now this county. The militia  were  summoned formed into line ready for draft.  They did not like to go so far to fight Indians.  But just before the "hat" was passed, an order came to give a chance for volunteers. Enough volunteered to make up the company, and a shout of joy rang out along the line from those who did not want to go, on seeing the company full, Hugh, Samuel, Thomas, Jackson and James Parks, Junior Meredith, Wm. Crain, Wm. Groves and O. H. Wiley, were among the number who went. Obadiah West was elected Captain; Hugh Parks First Lieutenant, and Robert West Second Lieutenant. They went through to Rock river on horseback, and after three months returned home without having done any fighting. Black Hawk was defeated, and soon after died.

The division of Franklin county into the counties of Franklin and Williamson, was authorized by Act of Legislature, approved February the 28th, 1839, providing that the legal voters of Franklin county should meet at their respective places of voting, on the first Monday in August, 1839, and vote for or against a division of the county. The Act further provided that in case a majority of the votes cast were in favor of division, the new county should be called "Williamson," and then proceeded to bound the county. The election was held, and a majority voted for the division. The Act also provided that an election for county officers should be held on the first Monday in September, 1839, and the returns of said election should be made to Wm. Norris, Starling Hill, and John T. Davis, three Justices, who should meet at Bainbridge, and abstract the returns, and transmit the same to the Secretary of State. This election resulted in the election of Duncan and Hill, as County Commissioners; Campbell was already one by virtue of being one in Franklin county. Sanders was elected Sheriff. The Act also provided for a division of the school funds, and Williamson county got $469.51, as her part. By the same Act, Calvin Bridges, of Union county, Thornsberry C. Anderson of Gallatin, and Jefferson Allen, of Jackson, were appointed to locate and lay out the seat of Justice in this county. They were authorized to require a donation of twenty acres of land, to be made to the county, for this purpose. On the 19th day of August, 1839, the commissioners appeared before Wm. Norris, and took an oath to locate the county seat as near the center of the county as was eligible.

On the 7th day of October, 1839, the County Commissioners met at the residence of Wm. Benson, and cast lots for the different terms of service. Campbell drew

the short term, one year; Hill, the interme-
diate, and Duncan the long term, three
years. Their first work was to approve the
bond of the Sheriff and County Clerk. On
the same day, October 8th, John Davis reported as Justice of the Peace, of having
fined Thos. Culbreth $3.00 for an assault
and battery on Michael Shanks, which is
the first criminal case recorded in the county. Two days afterward, the Court laid the
county off into five election precincts,
Northern, Saline, Grassy, Fredonia and Marion, which extended through the county
north and south; and appointed Judges of
Election. They then laid the county out in
twelve road districts, corresponding to our
twelve townships, and appointed Supervis-
ors. Men were also appointed to mark out
and locate roads. Henry W. Perry surveyed
the town lots. These were ordered to be
sold on six, twelve and eighteen months'
time by the Sheriff. The sale commenced
on the 17th day of November, 1839, and continued for three days, during which time
thirty-eight lots were sold, and went very
high.

The southeast corner of the square was
covered with a heavy growth of hazel brush,
and R. M. Hundley, Daniel Stroud and Jesse

Sanders were employed to "shrub off" the square.

On the second day of December, 1839, Gabriel Sanders took the contract for building the Clerk's office on the square, for $108. It was finished, and the Court moved into it May the 4th, 1850. The contract for the jail was let to Squire Howell, for $335, on the 8th day of January, 1840. It was a log house, and stood where the jail now stands. When he got it finished the Court docked him $25, for defective work.

Richard Cook was the first prisoner. He had been in Franklin jail from this end of the county on a charge of horse stealing, before the division, and brought here. John G. Sparks was first Jailer, and got thirty-seven and a half cents a day for dieting prisoners.

John Davis was the first man to get license to retail whisky; but during 1839, two of the County Court began to sell whisky. A pretty hard record for this county. Campbell kept at Bainbridge, and Hill at his residence, until he moved to Marion, and the "Honorable the Worshipful" Judges fixed the price of whisky at twenty-five cents a pint, which they afterwards reduced to twenty and a half cents.

On the 3rd day of March, 1840, the

Court divided the county into two Assessor's districts. Western, with Samuel T. Russell, Assessor, and Eastern, with George W. Binkley. At the first assessment there were 154 tracks of land, valued at $27,136. Personal property was valued at $139,410. Taxes on land was twenty and on personal property twenty-five cents per hundred dollars' worth. Total taxes for 1839, $749.25; delinquent list, $18.01 1-2; $407.12 of this amount was county funds. The Clerk received two cents a tract for extending the land on the Collector's books, $3.08, and five per cent. on personal property, $69.70.

In 1841, John Paschal built the courthouse. It was forty feet square, two stories high, and built of brick, on the Square, at a cost of $3,500. It stood until 1859, when it was removed and a house built of the brick on the Brooks farm.

March 3rd, 1840, the first grand and petit jury were selected by the Court; only three of the first are alive—O. H. Wiley, Hugh Parks, and Thomas Cox; and only two of the last—L. C. Parks and James Shaw. During this year the Court appointed Overseers of the Poor, and up to 1860, when the county bought the poor farm, there were a great many sickly people in the county. Ehud Lamaster took the contract to keep the paupers, at $1.40 per week, per head. There were not one-tenth as many. They did not like to be sick, but the idea of going to the poor house was intolerable. The house cost $147. The keepers have been Lamaster, Roberts, Cash and Doty. One of the paupers, Rebecca Hilderbrand, has been a county charge for twenty-three years and has cost the county $2,392.

In 1840, Warrington K. Spiller transcribed the land records of Franklin county, pertaining to this county, for $46. The county records are now all in a perfect condition; but some of them are badly written and difficult to read. The first Circuit Court was began May 4, 1840, by Walter B. Scates, in the little clerk's office on the Square. This court was conducted very loosely. A Justice's court had simply authority, without dignity, in those days.

While Starling Hill was County Commissioner, he was also ex-officio a Justice of the Peace, and kept a grocery in Marion. He could be seen sitting at his window, selling whisky to a fighting rabble on the outside, while a case was being tried on the inside by a jury, and the jury, lawyers, witnesses and everybody else half drunk, talking about horse races, etc., so mixed up that nobody could tell the jury from the rabble; but when the verdict came, it was about right. This was not the case in Hill's court alone, but it was the general custom.

Under the law of 1819, the Court had power to fix the fare at hotels, and they fixed the price of a meal at 12 cents, of horse-feed at 12 cents, and of lodging at 6 1-4 cents.

Allen Bainbridge put up the "Western Exchange," the first regular hotel in the town. It was a brick building, fifty feet long, and two stories high, situated on the north side of the Square, on which he paid out 37 1-2 cents in cash, the rest being paid in goods. In 1844, there were four Abolitionists in the county, and three hundred Whigs. Political excitement ran very high. Some of the Democrats had the horns of their oxen painted with polk berries, and one teacher brought his whole school into town, with his scholars painted. The Whigs would drag the polk stalk in the dust behind their wagons, and the result was many fights. I tell this to show that thirty years progress has made us no better. The Cutrells, Russells, Roberts, Ryburns and McDoonalds were Whigs. The first liberty-pole raised in the county, was raised in 1848, by the Whigs.

—F 16

When the call for troops was made to fight Mexico, this county responded promptly. In 1846, A. P. Corder and E. A. Phillips took a few men from this county. and entered the service at Calendonia, Illinois. They joined Capt. H. L. Webb's company, in the 2d regiment of the first call of Illinois Volunteers. On the battle-field of Beuna Vista, Corder was promoted to the rank of a captain, from a private, for his reckless bravery. In 1847, John M. Cunningham made up a company of one hundred and twenty-five men, and left Marion, May the 24th, for Alton. On arriving there, Jackson Damron took forty of the men and joined company "E," from St. Clair county. Cunningham's company was Company "B," of the first regiment of the second call, or 5th Illinois regiment. B. F. Furlong was First Lieutenant, R. M. Hundley was Second Lieutenant, and D. L. Pully was Third Lieutenant, W. H. Eubanks, Orderly Sergeant; Wm. Sykes, Chief Musician; Harvey Russell. Color-bearer; E. W. B. Nubia (a very bad man), was Colonel, and —— Boykin (a very good man), Lieutenant-Colonel. They left Alton June 17th, 1847; left Leavenworth, July 7th, and marched through to Santa Fe on foot, where they arrived December 12. They returned home October,

1848, and were received with public dinner in the Court House.

Capt. James Hampton raised another squad in this county, and joined John A. Logan from Jackson, and one Provo, from Union, and made another company. Thomas I. McKinney, now General McKinney, was a private in Cunningham's company. A soldier, in 1848, in this county, was a curiosity, and the people came from all quarters to see the troops, as they returned home.

In 1852, J. M. Campbell was appointed Drainage Commissioner, to sell the swamp lands of the county, but he soon resigned, and James D. Pully was appointed in his place. In 1863, Mr. Pully made his full report, having sold all the swamp lands of the county, amounting to over 23,000 acres. These lands were sold in 1st, 2nd and 3rd classes, for 75, 50 and 25 cents per acre, and the proceeds went to the school fund.

During the campaign of 1856, the Democrats were very noisy, and the Republicans were silent. Griffin Garland made the first Republican speech in the county, during this campaign, and Col. Ben L. Wiley, Republican candidate for Congress, received forty-four votes in the county. The campaign of 1856 was attended by many rough-and-tumble fights, and whisky was issued out by the bucket full. Men were generally allowed to vote as they pleased, but abolitionists were looked upon with contempt.

On the 19th day of March 1858, R. M. Hundley took the contract of building a new court-house for $9,500, $7,700 in county orders, and $1,800 out of the swamp land fund. He gave bond in the sum of $19,000 to have it completed by the 15th day of November 1858, which he did. He then got $245 for painting it, and N. B. Colvert $305 for furnishing the court room. It was burned down May 30, 1875. All the houses on the block on which it stood were also burned, the loss being about $25,000. This was the only fire that ever occurred in Marion of any consequence.

The old court-house was a plain, brick building, without any parapets, turrets or ramparts. Many have been the scenes of revelry and romance within its courts. Its walls have resounded with the commotion of war-like preparations, and the still, poisonous breath of treason has been whispered in its precincts. Again, it has been the scene of festive occasions, where our native belles vied with other in a perfect oreola of beauty. Lot No. 2 of block No. 5 of the original survey, on which this house stood, was sold by the county June 19, 1875, for $1,775.

The court then rented a room from Goodall and Camp'bell, for $500 a year, to hold court in. At the November election of that year, a proposition was submitted to the voters for raising, by special taxation, a sum sufficient in five years to build a courthouse; but the majority was against it.

The first politician that figured in our county was Thomas Roberts, of Northern. He was a member of the Constitutional Convention of 1818. Willis Allen and Allen Bainbridge were both elected in 1838, to the Legislature on the question of a division of the county. Soon after the division, Allen moved to Marion, and bought three acres land from Benson. It had a log cabin on it, in which he lived for some time. He was a man of considerable talent, great shrewdness, and un'bounded energy. He lived respected by all, and idolized by his party. He went to Congress in 1852, again in 1854, served several terms in the Legislature, and died in 1859, while holding court, as circuit judge, in Saline county. Allen was a spare built man, erect, graceful, and of uncommon strength, agility and endurance. His voice was soft and melodious, countenance rudy and fair, his hair was russet brown, a soft grayish blue eye, lighted by a fascinating smile. He was frank, generous and confiding to a fault, and was more interested in doing a kindness to others, than serving himself.    When he was engaged his glance was withering.    He was the father of the Honorable W. J. Allen, and was    the    most powerful politician in Southern Illinois in his day.

In 1848, John T. Lowden was a member of the Constitutional Convention from this county.    He was a Whig, but    a    man    of prominence and    merit.    The    Ingersolls came to this county about 1853, and in 1854 Robert J. and Clark, and W. J. Allen    were all admitted to the bar.    They were considered a very intellectual family; but, being Abolitionists, and the boys being deists, rendered them obnoxious to our people in that respect.    Robert and J. H. Manier, on one occasion, got the keys to the printing office, and one night went in and printed a long poem, which Robert had    written,    on    the citizens of the town, and left a copy at each man's door.    The poem was    abusive,    and created a considerable stir, but the author could never be found.    Robert    once    got mad at Josh. Allen for something, and used to say on the streets, "I    will    overshadow Josh. Allen yet."    They left here in 1856, and settled at Peoria, and Robert J. Ingersoll is now one of the most renowned orators of ancient or modern times.

Anderson P. Corder was known in Franklin county as a school teacher. He came to Marion in 1840, and commenced the practice of law. He figured in our politics until 1874, and was the most singular politician ever in the county. Sometimes he would rise in public estimation until he could have been elected to and office; then, again, sink beneath public contempt. He was in the State Senate one term, and held the position of Master-in-Chancery. He was not a profound thinker, but a witty, fluent speaker. From 1840 to 1850, he held almost despotic political influence. No man thought of running for office without his consent; but in latter years he lived a hard, intemperate life, and not only lost his influence, but lost that respect which ought to attend a man of gray hairs. There are many incidents in the life of this man that would be interesting to our people, had I room to give them. During the war he was an outspoken southern sympathizer, but when invasion threatened this State, he drew his sword for defense.

Hon. W. J. Allen was raised in this county, was in Congress several terms, and in the Legislature. He moved to Cairo in

1865, and now resides in Carbondale. For the last twenty-two years he has been intimately connected with our politics, and appears conspicuous and interesting at every point. He was for a long time a law partner of Senator John A. Logan, when he (Logan) lived in this county. The characters of these men are not local, and therefore not a part of my subject, only where they have operated in our local politics. They are both men whose profound and universal genius it is impossible to contemplate without respect. And, however much we may differ from either of them politically, we are bound to admit that they are great men—the honor and pride of our county. Our children will proud that such men ever lived in the county.

Capt. John M. Cunningham, the father-in-law of John A. Logan, was a politician of good ability; one of the most affable and polished men of his day. He held several county offices, and, like Corder, was a Democrat, and during the war, very bitter. In 1869 he received the appointment of Provost Marshal in Utah Territory, where he died in 1874, and was brought to Marion by Mrs. Mary Logan.

James D. Pully was a leader in the Democratic party during the war, and a man of fine personal appearance, and a high order of intelligence. He served two terms in the Legislature, and was Lieutenant-Colonel of the One Hundred and Twenty-Eighth Regiment of Illinois Volunteers. His outspoken manner of defending his principles was the cause of some personal feelings between him and Republicans. He died January 2nd, 1866, in the full vigor of manhood.

Colonel Robert M. Hundley came into this county in 1838, a penniless boy, and is now one of our wealthiest citizens. He is a man of talent and great shrewdness. During the war he was an ardent Democrat, wielded a powerful influence. He was Colonel of tne One Hundred and Twenty-Eighth Illinois Volunteers, and in 1868 came out as a Republican candidate for State Senator, 'but was defeated. Since then he has held the balance ot power between the two parties in this county, and generally uses it on the side of the Democracy. He is a very outspoken, fluent talker, but does his political work sub rosa, so that the effect can be seen like the bursting up of waters from an undercurrent. He still lives in this county, as a target for the deliberate and persistent defamation of his

opponents, and the spontaneous praise of
his admirers.

George W. Goddard is a lawyer and politician of the old stripe and fashion—too
honest for modern politics. He is a War
Democrat, and was Captain of Company
C, Thirty-First Regiment Illinois Volunteers. In the army he was a brave and respected soldier. He has been Circuit Clerk,
and is now Mayor of Marion, and is one
of those men "in whom the elements are so
happily united that Nature can stand up
and say to all the world, this is a man."

Hon. A. C. Nelson came to this county
over twenty-five years ago, penniless. As
a partisan, he is a Democrat, and is a man of
good talent, and very eloquent. He served
one term in the Legislature, and won for
himself the title of "Egyptian orator." Mr.
Nelson has served his party well, and now
lives on his farm, a model of all that is honorable in principle, virtuous in nature, and
praisworty in action. He is a minister
who practices what he preaches, and will
live in our history in an immortality of respect.

James M. Washburn commenced the
practice of law in this county fifteen years
ago, and since been a Democratic politician
of considerable prominence. During the

war he was very bitter at times, and has been elected to the State Senate, and also to the Lower House, in 1876, and as a member of the Constitutional Convention in 1869. He is a man that all parties admit is honest and upright in his daily work, and is now the leader of his party.

Jesse Bishop, a leading Republican, came into this county during the war, and has since held a high place in our politics. He several times fared roughly at the hands of Democrats, but managed to carry a good many of them with him when he was elected County Judge.

William W. Clemens, a leading Democrat, is a man of excellent talent, and, though a man of delicate constitution, has great tenacity of life, and physical endurance. He walked into this county in 1862; a poor boy, without money, and commenced the study of law, and has since worked his way up to the highest room in the public estimation. He possesses a boyant and happy temperament, lives a pure life, fond of home and the society of his friends. He cares but little for the bitter invectives of crafty demagogues. What he is and what he has, are the legitimate results of persistent labor, backed by economy and good sense. His solid legal attainments have won for him the respect, and placed him in the foremost rank, of the bar in Southern Illinois.

John H. Mulkey commenced the practice of law in this county in 1856, and soon removed to Cairo, where he is to-day acknowledged to be the most profound and classic lawyer in all of Egypt.

George W. Young, a lawyer and leading Republican, was raised in this county. His early life was rendered unpleasant by poverty and frequent hardships. He enlisted in the army when a mere boy, and rose to the rank of lieutenant. He belonged to that class of men who would "rather be right than President," and his unobsequious, self-directed attachment to what he believes to be honest and right, makes him appear abrupt and independent; thereby rendering him unpopular with those who do not share his opinions; but as a citizen and officer his conduct is emblazoned by the highest morability and integrity.

Jerome B. Calvert, a leading lawyer and Democrat, is a man whose life has been marked by the highest integrity, but, owing to his indisposition to ingratiate himself into popular favor, by simulating graces and deceptive smiles, he has not reached the prominence in his party that his ability and honesty entitle him to.

Some of the men whom I have described were the politicians in the great campaign of 1860.   Nobody in this county ever dreamed that Abraham Lincoln would be elected President; and though there were less than one hundred Republicans in the county, yet the excitement ran higher than usual. When Lincoln was elected, many of  our  people felt it their duty to stand by him.  John  A. Logan openly declared that he would shoulder his gun to have him inaugurated.  The people commence to change over to the Republican party before Lincoln took  his seat. They first declared for the Union, then endorsed General Scott, and finally Abraham Lincoln.  But among the old-liners a strong sympathy for the South was felt·  By  the first of April, 1861, the parties were nearly equally divided, and excitement was  running very high.  Our leading men were  in trouble, and some were noisy and clamorous for Southern Rights.  In a few days after the inauguration, Peter  Keifer made a speech in the Court House, in which he said, "Our Country Must Be Saved;" but it was understood that "our  country"  meant the South,, by the motion of his hand. Sympathy of "our Southern brethren"  became

stronger and stronger every day.  Proposi-
tions for organizing the  people into  companies and regiments were made. Secession
was openly talked of until the 9th day of
April, 1861, when it began to take shape. It
was just after the fall of Fort Sumpter; a
party of ten or fifteen men got together  in
a saloon in Marion, and agreed to call a public meeting to pass ordinances of secession.
They appointed a committee on resolutions,
who were to report at the public meeting.
The call was made for a meeting to be held
in the Court House, on Monday, April 15th,
1861, to provide for the "public safety." A
large crowd came in, and the meeting  was
called to order, and James D. Manier elected
President.  He then appointed  G.  W. Goddard, James M. Washburn, Henry C. Hooper, John M. Cunningham, and Wm.  R. Scurlock, a committee to draft resolution of secession.  The saloon committee had the resolutions already prepared, and they  were reported and passed with but one dissenting
voice, and that was A. T. Benson, and were
as follows:

*Resolved,* That we, the citizens of Williamson county, firmly believing,  from the
distracted condition of our country, the same
being brought about by the elevation to power of a strictly sectional party, the coercive

policy of which toward the seceded States will drive all the border Slave States from the Federal Union, and cause them to join the Southern Confederacy.

*Resolved*, That, in that event, the interest of the citizens of Southern Illinois imperatively demands at their hands a division of the State. We hereby pledge ourselves to use all means in our power to effect the same, and attach ourselves to the Southern Confederacy.

*Resolved*, That, in our opinion, it is the duty of the present administration to withdraw all the troops of the Federal Government that may be stationed in Southern forts, and acknowledge the independence of the Southern Confederacy, believing that such a course would be calculated to restore peace and harmony to our distracted country.

*Resolved*, That in view of the fact that it is probable that the present Governor of the State of Illinois will call upon the citizens of the same to take up arms for the purpose of subjugating the people of the South, we hereby enter our protest against such a course, and, as loyal citizens, will refuse, frown down and forever oppose the same.

These resolutions were written by Henry C. Hooper. The Republicans of this county used to accuse the Hon. W. J. Allen of drafting them, on account of the peculiar phraseology; but in this they were wrong. The news of this meeting spread rapidly, and by the next morning it had reached Carbondale, and had been telegraphed to Gen. Prentiss, at Cairo. The people of Carbondale, seeing the trouble our people were bringing on themselves, sent J. M. Campbell up to Marion on the 16th of April, to tell the people to revoke the resolutions. Ite said they must be repealed, or war would be brought on our soil and at our own doors. The people were exicted badly. A meeting was called to repeal the resolutions, and to meet instanter, but not by the same men who were in the meeting of the 15th. W. J. Allen was called in to address the meeting, which he did at some length. He said he was for repealing the resolutions, and that others could do as they pleased, but as for him and his house, they would stand still and see the salvation of the Lord.

The resolutions were repealed, and A. T. Benson appointed a committee of one to convey a copy of the proceeding to Gen. Prentiss. When he arrived at Cairo he found Gen. Prentiss reading the resolutions.

He gave him a copy of the proceedings of the meeting of the 16th, and Prentiss said, "I am glad to see them. The resolutions of secession would have caused your folks trouble; but I hope all will be right."

John A. Logan was not in the county when these meetings were held, and had not been for several days. This is a fact well known in this county. But it was charged against Gen. Logan in 1866, that he was present at, and aided in, the meeting of the 15th, and endorsed the resolutions. This charge was made by some unprincipled man outside of Williamson county. No such charge was ever made in this county, neither by Democrats nor Republicans; but, on the contrary, when the charge was made against Gen. Logan, nine of his political enemies, all prominent men, who were conspicuous at that meeting, volunteered their testimony against the truth of the charge; and one of them was James D. Manier, the President. The Democrats of this county knew that the charge against him was false, and they went to his rescue, and published to the world the evidence of its falsity. These men did not want to break Gen. Logan down by withholding truth or circulating falsehoods on him. It would not be an exhibition of merit in them, or hon-

—F 17

orable action. Those men who held the meeting of the 15th, contended that the meeting of the 16th had no right to repeal the resolutions, and that they were not repealed, and that the people must organize. So, a meeting was called to meet on the 27th of April, pursuant to the one of the 15th. The meeting was called to order, and a motion made to "seize the money in the hands of the Sheriff to defray the expenses of arming and equipping soldiers for the Southern Army." The fever for organizing into military companies had cooled off, so that this motion was lost, and the meeting broke up in a row. John A. Logan, who had come home, told the participants in these meetings that "the resolutions were treason, and they would all be hung," and they got scared and sent men out in the country to tear down the "Notices to Organize," which had been stuck up. But excitement continued to increase, and party feeling to deepen, and leading Democrats began to look upon Logan with suspicion, and accuse him of being a "turn-coat." In defense of himself he said that he would suffer his tongue to cleave to the roof of his mouth, and his right arm to wither and fall palsied by his side, before he would take up arms against his Southern brethren, unless it was to sustain the Government; and that if the war was prosecuted solely for the purpose of freeing negroes, he would not ground his arms, but would turn and shoot them North. Logan at this time was against the Abolitionists, but this opposition was lost in his terrible opposition to treason and traitors.

Gen. Prentiss had dropped off a company of men at Big Muddy bridge as he was going to Cairo; this was intolerable to our people; the whole country was in a flame. Thorndike Brooks and Harvey Hays raised the whoop in Marion; runners were sent out all over the county to tell the people to come into town next morning with their guns. Next morning a great many people came into town with guns, anxious to know what was wanted with them, when they were told that "the men at the bridge must be whipped away." Most of them turned and went home. Some objected, and said they had no guns, and that the soldiers had good guns, but some few went on to Carbondale, and others tried to get them not to go. At Carbondale, they found a noisy crowd assembled for the same purpose. Soon after they met they sent Isaiah Harris up to the bridge, which was four miles north of Carbondale, to spy around. When he got in sight of the soldiers he saw a cannon, and returned and told them that they could not whip the soldiers. News of these proceedings having reached Gen. Prentiss at Cairo, an hour before, he sent up another company, with more cannon. The train stopped at Carbondale, when the crowd was at its highest and most clamorous condition. After staying there awhile, she pulled on up to the bridge. At this crisis, Gov. Dougherty, W. Hecker, of Cairo and Gen. I. N. Hannie made speeches to the people, and told them to stand by the Union. Gov. Dougherty said, "that the speeches and guns persuaded the people not to attack the bridge." The people of Marion were standing listening for a bloody battle, but they were disappointed. A few straggling crowds came back from Carbondale, cursing and frothing like wild men. Wm. Crain swore he could have taken his boys and cleaned out the soldiers, and Brooks and Wheeler called the people cowards and slaves.

In two or three days after the Muddy bridge raid, which was about the 30th of April, John A. Logan, George W. Goddard, John H. White and John M. Cunningham, neither of whom was in the raid, met in secret caucus in White's office, and they solemnly pledged each other their honor that they would stand by the Union. They agreed that Logan should go on to Congress, and after he returned home they would raise a regiment of Union soldiers, of which he was to be Colonel, John H. White, Lieutenant Colonel, and Goddard was to be Captain; and White the County Clerk, were both to appoint Cunningham deputy to run the offices, and he was to be for the Union. This agreement was faithfully carried out by all parties concerned; but Cunningham continued to sympathize strongly with the South.

In a few days after the meeting, some one reported having seen eighteen soldiers in the tall grass near town. They raised a general uproar. Nobody knew what to do to save the town. Finally John H. White told the people that there was but one salvation, and that was to hoist the flag. In a few minutes the Star-Spangled Banner was seen waving against the sky. After Stephen A. Douglas made his Union speech, his liberty pole was cut to the ground in Marion, with some ceremony; and this was the first time a flag had been displayed. As soon as the excitement subsided, the flag was taken down. There never was but one rebel flag displayed publicly in this county, and that was about the first of June, 1861, at one of Charley Goodall's barbecues, four miles east of Marion.

On the 24th day of May, 1861, Colonel Brooks and Harvey Hayes, despairing of raising an army here, or organizing the county, formed the design of raising a company and going South. They sent a man to Carbondale to recruit, and they commenced at home. By the next evening they had about thirty names on their list, and had given orders for them to rendezvous at the "Delaware Crossing," on the Saline, six miles south of Marion. They all got to the place about two hours by sun, on the 25th of May, 1861, and the few that came from Carbondale swelled the number to thirty-five men, mostly under the age of twenty-three years. They started on to Paducah on foot, and walked all night; and next day in the afternoon Robert Kelly went on to Linn's Hotel to have supper prepared for the boys. The number had now increased to about forty men. Their feet became sore, and all of them lagged behind but six, who went on to get supper, where they were surrounded by 135 home-guards and taken prisoners. A friend to the boys got on his horse, knowing that they were coming into the same trap, and went up the road to let them know. The home-guards left a guard

with the six boys and came on up the road
to meet the others from Marion, but  when
they came to the forks of the road, north of
Linn's Hotel, supposing the boys had taken
the one leading to Brooklyn, started down to
the river.  The boys went on until they came
to the forks of the road, and seeing by the
tracks, that the guards had  gone  the  left
hand, they went on rapidly to Linn's Hotel,
where they re-captured their  six  companions, and went on to the river opposite Paducah.  Here Kelly had prepared a  ferry-
boat for them, but it had laid there twenty-
four hours, and the boilers had cooled off.
They were in a critical condition; but just
then saw a steamboat, the "Old Kentucky,"
rounding up to Paducah out of the mouth of
the Tennessee, and pretty soon they saw her
heading across the Ohio.  They boarded her,
and crossed the river.  They went to Mayfield, Kentucky, and joined Company "G,"
One Hundred and Fifthteenth Regiment of
Tennessee Volunteers, and were in General
Cheatham's command.

At the close of the war, about  half  of
them returned home.  Brooks got to be a
Lieutenant-Colonel, and is now  a  wealthy
merchant in Baltimore, Maryland.  It has
been repeatedly charged on John A. Logan,
that he assisted in raising the Company of

men to go South. This is not true. He was not in the county at the time, and neither he, nor W. J. Allen had anything to do with their going South. They were neither of them consulted, or gave any encouragement to the enterprise. In fact, no leading man in the county knew anything about it until they were gone.

In 1866, a man by the name of John Wheatley filed an affidavit in Cairo, in which he said that he was personally advised to join this company by John A. Logan, and that he left Williamson county with the company, and that John A. Logan went with them as far as Paducah, and left them, promising to return to them. And that the next time he saw Logan was at Belmont, where he chased him so closely that Logan dismounted, and he got his horse. This man Wheatley simply swore falsely. He was not a citizen of this county, and never has been, and he is unknown to our people. There is not a soldier of that company in this county but will state that Wheatley swore fasely in every respect concerning Logan.

W. M. Davis, one of the soldiers in this company, and one who was badly wounded at Shiloh, also filed an affidavit that he joined this company under the (advice) influence of John A. Logan. Mr. Davis has

been a citizen of this county for twenty-one
years, and is now the City Marshal of the
city of Marion. When he made this affidavit he lived in Equality, Illinois. He says
he did not think of going into the Confederate Army until a few days before he started. Logan was not here at that time, and of
course could not advise him to go. William
M. Davis is thirty-five years old and a very
sober, honest, and respectable, and in every
way an exemplary and trustworthy citizen.
He is now at this moment sitting by my side
and dictating to me what to write, and every
word concerning his affidavit in this book
is written by his consent and dictation. He
says that they got his affidavit wrong, in
this, that they put into it the word "advice."
He says that he did not swear nor mean that
John A. Logan ever advised him, or any
other man, to go into the Southern Army,
and he says that Logan never did speak to
him on that subject in his life, or to any other man in his presence or hearing. He says
that what he meant was this, that Logan
being a man of great influence in this county, and he believed that his sympathy was
with the South, and in this way Logan influenced him to go South. Or, in other
words, he believed so strongly at that time
that Logan's sympathy was with the South

that the supposed political position thus attributed to him by this belief, caused Logan's
influence to effect him in such  a  manner
that in going South to fight, he felt that he
had, as a warrant to back his actions,  the
connivance and friendship of  Logan,  and
that this is all he knows about Logan's disloyalty.  Mr. Davis says that Wheatley got
with the company at  Mayfield,  Kentucky,
and was not from this county, and that he
swore falsely in every particular concerning
Logan.  He is a strong Democrat, but a man
of discretion and firmness, and stands up
for what he believes to be right in principle
and conduct.

Col. Brooks wrote a letter to Gen. Logan
in which he said that Logan had nothing to
do with the recruiting or sending off of any
of his men. Hibert B. Cunningham, afterward captain of the company, A. H. Morgan,
W. R. Tinker and Joshua Lowe, all soldiers
in that company in 1866, certified that Logan had nothing to do directly or indirectly
with any of the men going  South.  Also
John M. Cunningham, R. J.  Pully,  G.  C.
Campbell, George W. Lowe, B.  F.  Lowe,
William Cook and D. L. Pully, all  at that
time prominent citizens of Marion, certified
that they were cognizant of all the circumstances attending the recruiting and sending

of the soldiers south to join the Confederate
Army, and that Logan had nothing to do
with it, or had any knowledge of it.

James D. Pully and M. C. Campbell went
to Paducah the day before the soldiers left
here, and it was charged that they were on
the "Old Kentucky" when she crossed the
Ohio. This charge got circulated, and when
Col. Pully, near a month afterwards, started
to Springfield as a grand juror, he was arrested at Carbondale on this charge and
taken to Springfield. Capt. A. P. Cordor,
who then lived at Carbondale, became alarm-
ed, and came up to Marion, where he arrived late in the afternoon. He told the
people about Pully's arrest and insinuated
that a company was coming up from Muddy
Bridge that night after Logan and Allen.
This produced the greatest excitement; the
people trembled at the dreadful crisis; they
commenced getting drunk, and by a half
hour by sun there were enough drunks to
make a considerable crowd. Logan took
command, and ordered them to report on the
square at dark.

About thirty-five reported, and when in-
quiries were made about "Josh," (Hon. W.
J. Allen,) Logan said, "I guess he is at home
under the bed. Go and bring him out. . . ."
Josh came out, and they took up their line

of march to the old Fair Grounds, a half
mile west of town, taking jugs and bottles,
in place of powder and guns. When they
arrived there, Logan gave Capt. G. W. Goddard his pistol (the only firearm in the
crowd,) and detailed him to stand guard at
the mile tree, and report the approach of the
enemy. He was to fire and fall back by the
'best route, firing all the while. About ten
o'clock their whisky gave out, and the main
body had to fall back to town for supplies.
After replenishing their depleted quartermaster, they struck up a line of march for
the Goodall bridge, one and a half miles
southeast of Marion, a locality conspicuous
at that time for other reasons.

About eleven o'clock the citizens in town
sent John H. White to Carbondale for a
"compromise." About the same hour, J. M.
Campbell and J. M. Prickett started from
Carbondale to come to Marion, to let the
people know that there was no danger. They
met on the road, but not recognizing
each other, did not speak. Campbell and
Prickett ran into the picket line about
twelve o'clock, and were halted and arrested by Goddard, who, when he saw who it
was, started on to town with them. Just
before this, the idea got into the heads of

the men at the 'bridge that they had not re-
lieved Goddard. So, R. M. Allen was detain-
ed as a courier—on account of the acute-
ness of his hearing—to go and call in the
pickets. He was on horseback, going on the
jump, when he saw Goddard and his friends
in the road. Thinking that it was the
enemy, he went back to the bridge under the
lash, and reported the enemy nearby. A
scene of wildest consternation prevailed. By
this time they had got two old shot-guns.
Logan made a desperate effort to rally his
men. Josh commanded one wing, and
rallied two. All that were sober enough fell
into line, and the rest would have done so if
they could. It commenced raining about
dark that night, and rained all night a steady
rain. Logan formed his line, composed of
about sixty men, and Josh formed his parallel, composed of about sixty men, armed
with clubs. The rest of the men were lying
around by logs and stumps, unable to muster
Logan told Josh not to form his men parel-
lel to his, as they would shoot into each other
that way; but Josh insisted that his line was
formed right. A dispute came up, and ended
in a regular pow-wow, and almost a great
battle. Josh withdrew his forces and struck
camp across the creek; but no enemy came.
The storm-cloud was piling its temples of

blackness over the dark hill. The pelting of the rain kept step with the music of the rippling stream in the glen below. The men were lying around, fast asleep, covered with mud, on beds of water. In this condition they were found by R. J. Pully, who was sent down by Goddard to let them know that no enemy was coming. Josh and his command left the field and went home. Logan retreated in good order to Marion with his squad. The rear was brought up next morning by Clemison, who went to old Negro Sam's and got breakfast. Thus was this splendid army cut to pieces and routed without the loss of a single man. Next day, others heard this tale of luxury, decided to have another meeting that night, which they did. About one hundred of them met on the creek, south of town, but there were too many smart men in the crowd, and they broke up in a row.

In a few days Logan went to Benton, and the county was again thrown into excitement by John A. McClernand sending a dispatch to John M. Cunningham, asking assistance in raising a brigade of soldiers. This was the first time that our folks knew that they would be called upon for troops. Cunningham consulted with his friends, and decided to not assist.

The first troops that were ever in this county were those of Col. Hobb's Third Illinois regiment of cavalry. They passed through the county from Bloomington, on their way to Paducah. They were a fine-looking set of men, and conducted themselves very gentlemanly. They camped at the Delaware Crossing. Gen. Logan was called to meet at Congress on the 4th of July, 1861, and after the great battle of Bull's Run, in which he took part, returned home in the latter part of August, and on the 3rd day of September, made his first speech in this county in raising his regiment; and on the 13th day of September the Thirty-first Illinois Volunteers was organized. Men kept going from this county into the regiment, and party feelings kept getting stronger, until a few words was sufficient to create disturbances. Republicans were very coolly received here in the latter part of 1861. P. H. Lang, the postmaster of Marion, and a Republican, was threatened, and he had to move the post-office to Bainbridge, where he kept it about six weeks. This was so inconvenient to the people of Marion that they offered protection to Lang if he would bring the office back. He did so, and the promise was always faithfully kept.

Political poison permeated nearly every mind and place. It got into the Church, and even raised its head in the sacred Temple of Justice.

At the June term of our Circuit Court, 1862, out of forty-seven jurors, only two were Republicans, and about the proportion in 1863-4. And when the Republicans carried the county, in 1865, this feeling was carried as far on the other side. Again, in 1869, when the Democrats carried the county, this feeling had not entirely died out, although all honest men had long been disgusted with it, and ashamed of it. Since 1870, no lawyer asks what a juror's politics are.

On or about the 14th day of August, 1862, A. D. Duff, W. J. Allen, A. P. Corder, John Clemison and A. C. Nelson were all arrested by United States officers, and taken to Cairo, where they were kept about three weeks and then taken to Washington, and kept in the Old Capitol prison for nearly three months, and then turned loose without trial. These parties were charged with making rebel speeches; with belonging to the Knights of the Golden Circle, and stirring up sedition and treason. They claimed that they had committed no overt act against the Government, or any other crime, and that while they thought the Knights of the Golden Circle was a good and loyal society, they did not belong to it. They denied making rebel speeches, but insisted that they were for peace. They were arrested on affidavits filed in the Provost Marshal's offices, in Cairo, charging them with these offenses, and the writ of habeas corpus being suspended by the President, of course they could not get a trial, although they repeatedly demanded one. After their release, Judge Duff published on the 15th day of December, 1862, an address to the people of South Illinois, "Relative to his arrest by the Abolition Despotism." It was a caustic and scathing letter. A regular diabolical slayer of marshals, detectives, police, etc. He claimed that they were arrested in order that the Republicans could carry the fall election. Their arrests had but little effect on the county. The people grew more turbulent, and personal difficulties became more frequent. At this time the Golden Circle was in the most flourishing condition. The design was formed in this Order of raising a regiment for the Union Army, for the purpose of repelling the imputation of disloyalty laid on some of its members.

R. M. Hundley and James D. Pully went to work, in August and September 1862, and

—F 18

raised the One Hundred and Twenty-Eighth Regiment Illinois Volunteers. There were some doubts whether the Governor would receive the regiment or not, and I. M. Lewis and G. L. Owen, Republicans, and A. T. Benson, Democrat, were sent to Springfield. At DuQuoin, they fell in with Dr. Burges, who went with them. He talked principally with Owen, and Benson became suspicious that Owen was not in good faith. Burges told Benson that the proposed officers for that regiment ought to be hung, and he ought to be arrested, and he did not know but what it would be done. Benson got scared at this, and wanted Lewis to return. Lewis said he was in good faith, and intended to go on. At Springfield, Lewis and Benson went to Harmon G. Reynolds, secretary of the Grand Lodge of Masons, and got a recommendation from him to the Governor. It was three days before they could get an audience with him. When they did get a hearing, Owen wanted Burges to do the talking, but Benson passed up his recommendations, and Yates asked him what they wanted. Benson stated the object of their visit, and their request was granted, and they dismissed. Benson said, "They were treated kindly by the finest-looking man on earth." After the regiment was raised, they went

into quarters for a few days at the Fair
Grounds; from here they went to Springfield, where they organized,   with  R.  M.
Hundley as Colonel, and James D. Pully as
Lieutenant-Colonel.   They remained there
about a month before they drew clothing,
and it was very cold, and they half naked.
The Republican press abused them without
mercy, and the officers were looked upon
with suspicion and contempt, and given no
chance to exhibit their loyalty.   They were
called the "Whang Doodle Regiment."   The
men became dissatisfied, and soon began to
desert; but after they drew clothes, half of
them were furloughed home.   The remainder escorted General McClelland to Cairo.
Those who had been furloughed home never
reported back. A few of the remaining pri-
vates were transferred to other regiments,
and the others discharged.  While at Cairo
George Aikin,  the  Quartermaster  of this
regiment, went over to Jeff. Thompson's
army, and proposed to assist them in cap-
turing Cairo.  He agreed that this regiment
should all understand it, and not fire  on
them.  He made two trips for this purpose,
and had a gentleman with him  one  time.
The last trip, a lieutenant from Thompson's
army came with him to view the situation.
The intention was for Aikin and his confed-

erate to post all the soldiers, and for
Thompson to send soldiers over and capture
the city. Aikin commenced his insidious
works of informing the 'boys of his plot.
About the first man he told it to was Dr.
J. Clemison. Clemison went immediately
and told Colonel Hundley all about the infamous plot, and Hundley indignantly vetoed
the whole thing. This regiment was composed of as good material as any in the service, but they were badly treated. The
Chaplain said: "That there were men in
this regiment that would have turned their
guns against the Government I have no
doubt, but the majority of them would have
made as good soldiers as lived, under favora-
ble circumstances.

In the spring of 1863, one company of
the Thirty-Fifth Iowa were stationed here
for a short time. They were paroled prisoners off military duty, said to be, and were
here to assist the enrollment officer, but the
county was not enrolled.

In July and August, 1863, Major Biers,
with the third battalion of the Sixteenth
Illinois Cavalry, was camped in the old Fair
Ground. He was sent here to arrest desert-
ers, suppress sedition, and enroll the county.
He put the town under martial law,, with
Capt. Wilcot as Provost-Marshal, who sta-

tioned guards on all the principal streets. They required some persons to take the oath before leaving town. W. J. Allen was asked to take the oath of allegiance, or remain in town inside the lines. He remained in town, and part of the time with a guard around his residence. He said he had taken the oath in Congress and was willing to do so again, but that to be forced to would be construed in the light that he was acting so as to make it necessary. The Republicans charged that he refused to swear allegiance to his county because he was for the South. Col Hundley refused to take the oath for a while, but he lived outside of the lines, and was forced to as a matter of convenience.

The Provost-Marshal issued an order that no man should sell whisky to the soldiers. One day one of them got drunk, and a man by the name of McDaniel was caught running the guard line with a jug. When captured, he said he got the whisky at Lowe's saloon. Wilcot ordered all Lowe's whisky to be thrown into the streets, and several barrels of that popular article were wasted. At the August Term, 1863, of the Circuit Court, George Aikin, then foreman of the Grand Jury, swore before that body that Biers and some of his men came to his house in the day-time, took him out and whipped him, and then tied his hands behind him to a long pole, and then left him in a grove of thick saplings. Upon this evidence Biers was indicted, and a bench warrant issued for his arrest, and placed in the hands of Sheriff Spencer, who executed it by his deputy, Alex. Manier, without any resistance. But Biers' men soon heard of his arrest, and they formed on the Square, and told the Sheriff that he must release Biers. Spencer said he could not do that, as he had a warrant, but that he could not fight a regiment. Biers then walked out. The soldiers had just started to leave the county, when the Grand Jury adjourned. Biers arrested Aikin, who, when he started off, halloed out to the people, "Now you see where your liberty has gone to." They took him to Springfield, where he remained about a month, then came home and got a good start, and ran away. He was a very mean man. I have elsewhere spoken of the "Aiken gang," of which he was the leader. Aiken might have got whipped but that United States soldiers did it is preposterous. While Wilcot was in town he made an order that no man but a soldiers should wear brass buttons on their clothes. This was a tag at the soldiers of the One Hundred and Twenty-Eighth, who were still wearing their uniforms. They cut the buttons off some of their coats. A good many soldiers from this county went into the Ninth, Sixtieth, one Hundred and Tenth Illinois Infantry, and a company was raised to guard Muddy Bridge, which served three months in 1862; and in 1863 a company of hundred days' men were raised in this county.

From first to last, this county furnished about two thousand soldiers, a larger per cent than any other county in the state.

A majority of our people were true to the Government, true to her traditions, and taught the world that they were liberal of their blood when the flag of their country was assailed. The campaign of 1865 was the hottest one ever known in this county. The soldiers had returned and swelled the strength of the Republican party up to a majority. The city, which had witnessed all the horrors of 1863-4, was now again the constant scenes of fights, riots and routs. The Republican politicians walked all over the county and the Democrats walked with equal vigor. It was during this canvass that Capt. Cunningham is reported to have said to a friend, "Come up and help me, they are trying to take my office away from me." The election came off, and the Republicans were successful. They attributed their success to

the return of the soldiery, and the Democrats attributed their defeat to the "boiling
of sorghum." For two or three days after the
election, the Republicans made themselves
scarce on the streets. One was seen run-
ing through the field and when accosted by a
friend, told him not to go up town, for the
whole Democratic party were on a drunk. It
was the first time that the county had ever
gone Republican, and the Democrats were
concerned about it. Some of them said it
was ruined; others threatened to leave it,
while one insisted that they had just as well
turn the paupers out to feed on wild grapes.

The commissions of the new County
Court were mislaid, somehow, so that they
were in danger of not getting them in time.
They charged the Democrats of suppressing
them in the post office, so that the old Court
would get to meet once more, and fix the sal-
aries. Jesse Bishop went to Springfield to
get the commissions, and he was told that
the commissions had been sent long ago. He
got certified copies and returned. On the
day that Court was to meet, in stepped the
new members with their certified copies,
and demanded the offices. They were giv-
en up without a word, and the original commissions soon produced. With the exception

of this, there has been but one charge of fraud in the elections of this county. That was in 1864. The Republicans accused the Democrats of stuffing the ballot box in Lake Creek Precinct; but I know nothing of the truth of the charge. At the June Term of the County Court, 1864, R. M. Hundley and Arthur Boyle contracted to build the jail for the sum of $9,000, which they built, and Lodge and Spencer painted it, in 1865, for $350.

The campaign of 1868 was carried on grandly in this county, by both parties. Reason was taking the place of violence, and the politicians got down to hard work. The county again went Republican Since then it has been very near evenly divided. People have laid aside their prejudices to a great extent, and the elections have been conducted as becomes freemen. No man has been whipped for opinion's sake. Sympathetic feelings have sprung up among our people. There is no social or religious ostracism on account of politics, but all work together harmoniously for the common good.

The campaign of 1876, in this county, was one of a vast scene of peace and friendship. The election, though strongly contested passed off without a single ripple of discord to ruffle the political sea.

The defaulters in this county have been as follows:

The first one was R. R. Hendrickson, Sheriff, in 1862, to the amount of $1,643.85; he paid most of it himself, and the rest was collected on his bond. In 1864, W. R. Scurlock, County Superintendent, defaulted in the sum of $750, which was paid by his bondsmen. James Cheneworth, County Treasurer in 1863, was a defaulter to a less amount, which was collected by suit on his bond. In 1875, J. D. F. Jennings was defaulter, as State's Attorney, of about $900. Suit is now pending on his bond. These were Democrats. In 1872, A. N. Owen, Sheriff, and a Republican, was defaulter in the sum of $5,000. All the county and school part he paid up, but suit is now pending on his bond for the State tax, or part of it.

The county has never adopted township organization, but has twice voted on the question. Once on the petition of G. W. Young in 1873, and once on the petition of James M. Duncan, in 1874. That is an improvement in county government that our people have not yet learned, but the day is not far distant when it will be adopted.

The county has several times funded her non-interest bearing debt.

In 1874 it was funded in fifty-dollar

bonds, running for five years, and there was
$8,482.40 funded at that time. For the year
ending September 1876, the total expendi-
tures of the county were $31,366.79, but this
was on account of the criminal trials. The
taxes collected for that year were about
$17,000. The county ought to be run on
$8,000 a year in peaceable times, exclusive
of the interest on railroad bonds; but it oft-
ener reaches $10,000 or $12,000.

With this I close the volume, hoping that,
that impartiality and correctness with which
I have tried to write it, may be accorded to
me as a defense against the displeasure of
those who find defects and omissions in it.
And if it serves to assist any of the people of this great state in forming a correct
estimate of the character of our people, and
interests the companions of my youthful
days, I shall be satisfied.

**THE END.**

# Trieste

Trieste Publishing has a massive catalogue of classic book titles. Our aim is to provide readers with the highest quality reproductions of fiction and non-fiction literature that has stood the test of time. The many thousands of books in our collection have been sourced from libraries and private collections around the world.

The titles that Trieste Publishing has chosen to be part of the collection have been scanned to simulate the original. Our readers see the books the same way that their first readers did decades or a hundred or more years ago. Books from that period are often spoiled by imperfections that did not exist in the original. Imperfections could be in the form of blurred text, photographs, or missing pages. It is highly unlikely that this would occur with one of our books. Our extensive quality control ensures that the readers of Trieste Publishing's books will be delighted with their purchase. Our staff has thoroughly reviewed every page of all the books in the collection, repairing, or if necessary, rejecting titles that are not of the highest quality. This process ensures that the reader of one of Trieste Publishing's titles receives a volume that faithfully reproduces the original, and to the maximum degree possible, gives them the experience of owning the original work.

We pride ourselves on not only creating a pathway to an extensive reservoir of books of the finest quality, but also providing value to every one of our readers. Generally, Trieste books are purchased singly - on demand, however they may also be purchased in bulk. Readers interested in bulk purchases are invited to contact us directly to enquire about our tailored bulk rates. Email: customerservice@triestepublishing.com

# You May Also Like

## Persecution and Tolerance: Being the Hulsean Lectures Preached Before the University of Cambridge in 1893-4

## Mandell Creighton

ISBN: 9780649669356
Paperback: 164 pages
Dimensions: 6.14 x 0.35 x 9.21 inches
Language: eng

## Report of the Second Annual Meeting of the Maryland State Bar Association, Held at Ocean City, Maryland, July 28-29, 1897

## Conway W. Sams

ISBN: 9780649724185
Paperback: 130 pages
Dimensions: 6.14 x 0.28 x 9.21 inches
Language: eng

# You May Also Like

# Second Year Language Reader

## Franklin T. Baker & George R. Carpenter & Katharine B. Owen

ISBN: 9780649587667
Paperback: 176 pages
Dimensions: 6.14 x 0.38 x 9.21 inches
Language: eng

# The Credibility of the Christian Religion; Or, Thoughts on Modern Rationalism

## Samuel Smith

ISBN: 9780649557516
Paperback: 204 pages
Dimensions: 5.83 x 0.43 x 8.27 inches
Language: eng

www.triestepublishing.com

# You May Also Like

ISBN: 9780649420544
Paperback: 108 pages
Dimensions: 6.14 x 0.22 x 9.21 inches
Language: eng

## 1807-1907 The One Hundredth Anniversary of the incorporation of the Town of Arlington Massachusetts

## Various

ISBN: 9780649194292
Paperback: 44 pages
Dimensions: 6.14 x 0.09 x 9.21 inches
Language: eng

## Biennial report of the Board of State Harbor Commissioners, for the two fiscal years commencing July 1, 1890, and ending June 30, 1892

## Various

www.triestepublishing.com

# You May Also Like

ISBN: 9780649199693
Paperback: 48 pages
Dimensions: 6.14 x 0.10 x 9.21 inches
Language: eng

**Biennial report of the Board of State Harbor Commissioners for the two fisca years. Commeneing July 1, 1884, and Ending June 30, 1886**

**Various**

ISBN: 9780649196395
Paperback: 44 pages
Dimensions: 6.14 x 0.09 x 9.21 inches
Language: eng

**Biennial report of the Board of state commissioners, for the two fiscal years, commencing July 1, 1890, and ending June 30, 1892**

**Various**

Find more of our titles on our website.  We have a selection of thousands of titles that will interest you.  Please visit

www.triestepublishing.com